How to read Egyptian hieroglyphs

How to Read

Egyptian Hieroglyphs

A STEP-BY-STEP GUIDE TO TEACH YOURSELF

Mark Collier and Bill Manley

New illustrations by Richard Parkinson

THE BRITISH MUSEUM PRESS

Published by The British Museum Press
A division of The British Museum Company Ltd
46 Bloomsbury Street, London WC1B 3QQ

First published 1998
Reprinted with corrections 1999
Eleventh impression 2003
Reprinted with corrections 2003
Reprinted 2004

A catalogue record for this book is available from the British Library

ISBN 0 7141 1910 5

Designed by Andrew Shoolbred
Typeset in Meridien by Nigel Strudwick, using hieroglyphs from the Cleo Font designed by Cleo Huggins. Extra diacritics and hieroglyphs by Nigel Strudwick.
Cover design by Harry Green

Printed and bound in Great Britain
by CPI Bath

Cover: Inscription on a ritual implement, dedicated by King Senwosret I to his ancestor King Mentjuhotep II. For an explanation of the inscription, see page 126. The Metropolitan Museum of Art, New York, acc. no. 24.21, Rogers Fund, 1924.

Contents

Introduction

The aim of this book is to enable you to read and enjoy the hieroglyphs and the language of ancient Egypt. It is chiefly aimed at those who have had no previous experience of reading hieroglyphs, but should also benefit others who would like to improve their knowledge in line with contemporary research. Above all, this is a practical guide: from the very beginning you will be introduced to genuine hieroglyphic texts, with full supporting explanations and study aids. In order to do this, we have concentrated on monuments in the British Museum, in particular the stelae (or funerary inscriptions) of Egyptian officials, as well as coffins, tomb scenes, and the famous Abydos King-list of Ramesses II. Each chapter introduces you to a new feature of the hieroglyphic script or the language, and ends with copies of inscriptions on which you can practise your skills. We believe this approach has a number of advantages.

First, by reading genuine ancient inscriptions from the first lesson, you can build up your familiarity with the tricks of the trade: everything here (from individual signs to whole inscriptions) is typical of the kind of monuments displayed, not just in the British Museum, but in museums throughout the world. Secondly, by reading these monuments, we hope you will feel a real sense of achievement at each stage of the book. Thirdly, concentrating on a coherent group of monuments will allow us to raise some important topics – such as the role of Osiris, god of the dead, and the Mysteries celebrated at his cult centre, Abydos – which will help you to understand the cultural background of these monuments.

Rather than cramming in unnecessary detail, we will give you plenty of practice in reading hieroglyphs, and introduce you to the most common features of the ancient Egyptian language as it appears on these monuments. This will give you a firm basis on which to build, if you later move on to study other genres of the wealth of texts which survives from ancient Egypt – literature, religious wisdom, royal decrees, or whatever.

This book has developed out of a course which we have been teaching since 1992. It was clear to us back then that the existing introductions to ancient Egyptian were either too brief or too detailed, and that there was a need for an up-to-date course adapted to the needs of beginners studying at home. We have taught the course in various guises for several groups and institutions: the University of London Centre for Extra-Mural Studies, the Egypt Exploration Society, the University of Glasgow, the Workers Educational Association, the Sussex Egyptology Society and the Thames Valley Egyptological Society at the University of Reading. At the Bloomsbury Summer School in particular, we have had the chance to introduce people to hieroglyphs in the hot-house of a single, concentrated week of study. This book owes a great deal to the constructive feedback of the students at all these venues, who have helped us (sometimes forced us!) to refine and clarify the text, and as a result it is much clearer and more accessible. Although it would be impossible to acknowledge so many by name, we are immensely grateful to each and every one of them for their enthusiasm and feedback, and for encouraging us in our belief that this book – and the approach it embodies – is a worthwhile project.

In developing this project into book form, we have had the good fortune to be able to draw on the knowledge and support of many people. At the British Museum, Vivian Davies, Keeper of Egyptian Antiquities, first brought the project to the attention of British Museum Press, and encouraged us to make use of Richard Parkinson's expertise in copying hieroglyphic monuments; Stephen Quirke freely shared his considerable knowledge of Middle Kingdom officialdom, as well as encouragement and the first round of drinks; as noted, we are especially grateful to Richard Parkinson for his outstanding line drawings. At Bloomsbury Summer School, we would like to thank the Director, Christopher Coleman, who allowed us carte blanche to develop language courses, and also his admirable staff for diligently keeping us all (tutors and students) alive. Several colleagues have helped us to teach hieroglyphs at the School: Ludwig Morenz, Toby Wilkinson, and especially José-Ramon Pérez-Accino, who is now a regular partner in our teaching. At the University of London Centre for Extra-Mural Studies, our grateful thanks are due to Tony Legge and Lesley Hannigan, who allowed us the freedom to develop the course as we saw fit, and also to Louise Lambe. Mark drafted his contributions to the book while a resident Fellow at All Souls College, Oxford, and completed them after his appointment to the School of Archaeology, Classics and Oriental Studies, University of Liverpool; he would like to acknowledge the support of both these institutions. His work on the language sections of the book has developed in tandem with his comprehensive undergraduate grammar course, *Introduction to Middle Egyptian*, which will be published separately.

We are grateful to the staff of the British Museum Press, not least for agreeing to take on such a complex book; above all our editor, Carolyn Jones, for her dedication and good humour in dealing with such a demanding project. We would specially like to thank Nigel Strudwick for undertaking the English and Egyptian typesetting, and Helen Strudwick for correcting proofs in Nigel's absence. Finally our thanks are due to Mark Mechan, who prepared the map of Abydos on page 55.

It is customary to add a final word about partners, but in the present case our love and genuine heartfelt thanks are due to our wives, Joanne Timpson and Kathy McFall, who have put up with us, and this project, for a long time. In particular, Joanne, as well as coping with the arrival of Oliver and a preoccupied husband, still found time to comment on the final draft.

Mark Collier
Bill Manley

Introduction to the Revised Edition

We have been astonished by how well our little book has been received. At the time of writing, sales of the English-language editions have exceeded 100,000 and translations have been made into several other languages. This is a striking demonstration of how many people are keen to experience for themselves the pleasure of reading ancient Egyptian hieroglyphs. Accordingly we are grateful that the British Museum Press has offered us the chance to make changes to the original text, within the confines of the original format. During the last four years we have received an enormous amount of constructive feedback which we have sought to collate and incorporate into a new edition. In this regard, we are especially indebted to our German and Spanish translators, Eva Ambros and José-Ramón Pérez-Accino respectively. The feedback has been overwhelmingly positive and enourages us to believe that our approach meets the needs of most of our readers. However, we have taken the opportunity to reword certain crucial sections, smooth out perceived inconsistencies, and correct the inevitable errors in the original text. We are most grateful to our Editor, Carolyn Jones, for her continuing good humour, and to the Production Controller, Bill Jones. Once again, the complex problem of typesetting English and Egyptian alongside each other was solved with aplomb by Nigel Strudwick.

Mark Collier
Bill Manley
January 2003

DEDICATION

For Oliver, whose arrival made our work on the final manuscript such an adventure!

Illustrations

The line drawings of the stelae reproduced in this book were drawn by Richard Parkinson, Department of Ancient Egypt and Sudan, British Museum. The scenes from the Middle Kingdom tombs at Meir are from A.M. Blackman, *The Rock Tombs of Meir*, vols I, II and III, Egypt Exploration Society, London 1914 and 1915; we are grateful to the Society for permission to reproduce them. The photographs on pages 31, 44, 63, 64, 108 and 125 are supplied courtesy of the Trustees of the British Museum, © British Museum Photography and Imaging Department. Mark Mechan prepared the map of Abydos on page 55.

Authors' note: Due to refurbishment work at the British Museum during 1997-8, it was not always possible for the authors to collate their own copies against the original monuments.

Chapter 1

Hieroglyphs

§1 Introduction

Hieroglyphs are pictures used as signs in writing. Many depict living creatures or objects (or their parts):

owl   seated man   mouth   water-pot

And, as you might expect, some signs represent the object they depict. So, for example, the mouth-sign is used to write the word for mouth, usually in combination with a stroke-sign (see §13 below for this sign):

r mouth

However, very few words are actually written in this way. Instead, hieroglyphic picture-signs are used to convey the *sound* (and meaning) of the ancient Egyptian language, just as the letters of our own alphabet convey the sounds of English. So, for example, the hieroglyphs above the figure roasting the goose do not read 'reed, chick, man, face' etc., which makes no sense; rather, they convey the sounds of various words in Egyptian which together have the following meaning:

'I have been roasting since the beginning of time – I have never seen the like of this goose' (Meir III, pl. 23)

The purpose of this book is to show you just how this is done.

§2 Reading hieroglyphs

How then can hieroglyphs be read to show us something of the sound of an ancient Egyptian word? The easiest way to see this is through looking at a real example. The sign  depicts a schematic house (in plan) and is used to write the word for 'house' as follows ( is the stroke-sign already noted above):

 *pr* house

As it happens, this word is based on the two consonants *p* and *r* combined to give *pr*. We shall discuss the way the ancient Egyptian word is put into our own writing system – how it is *transliterated* – in §§3 and 4 below. Now, there is another word which makes use of the same sound combination *p* and *r*, the word for 'go out', 'leave'. In hieroglyphs this is written as:

 *pr* go out, leave

In this word,  is no longer being used to depict a house, but rather to 'picture' the sound combination *pr* (this is discussed in Chapter 2). Put more formally,  is being used as a *sound-sign* or *phonogram*. This is termed the *rebus principle*; it is as if we were to write the English word *belief* with a picture of a bee and a leaf as . On this basis hieroglyphs can be used to indicate *sounds* rather than things and can thus be used in words quite unrelated in meaning to the objects they depict.

The word  *pr*, 'go out', also displays another two signs whose use will be explained more fully later. The mouth-sign reads *r* as it did in  *r* 'mouth', although it has nothing to do with 'mouth' here, being used instead to *complement* or clarify the reading of  *pr* (this is discussed in Chapter 2). The walking legs  are used as a *determinative*, a sign sometimes placed at the end of a word to give a general idea of its meaning, here of motion (see §6 below).

§3 Transliteration

In the last section we rendered  into our writing system as *pr*. It is the normal practice among Egyptologists to *transliterate* the sounds of a hieroglyphic word in this way. It is a very good discipline to get used to this right from the beginning and we encourage you always to transliterate when reading. The only real oddity about this is that hieroglyphs are not used to write vowels (a, e, i, o, u), only consonants; although this will seem a bit strange at first, you should soon get used to it.

§4 1-consonant signs

It is now time to get you started reading hieroglyphs for yourself. The most important hieroglyphs are the 1-consonant signs, where each hieroglyph contributes a single sound towards the reading of a word, rather like the letters of our own alphabet:

SIGN	TRANS-LIT.	SAY	SIGN	TRANS-LIT.	SAY	SIGN	TRANS-LIT.	SAY
𓄿	*ꜣ*	a	𓅓	*m*	m	𓈙	*š*	sh
𓇋	*ỉ*	i/a	𓈖	*n*	n	𓈎	*ḳ*	k
𓇋𓇋 or 𓏭	*y*	y	𓂋	*r*	r	𓎡	*k*	k
𓂝	*ꜥ*	a	𓉔	*h*	h	𓎼	*g*	g
𓅱 or 𓏲	*w*	w/u	𓎛	*ḥ*	h	𓏏	*t*	t
𓃀	*b*	b	𓐍	*ḫ*	kh	𓍿	*ṯ*	tj
𓊪	*p*	p	𓄡	*ẖ*	kh	𓂧	*d*	d
𓆑	*f*	f	𓋴 or 𓊃	*s*	s	𓆓	*ḏ*	j

We shall concentrate here on the reading of these signs. If you wish to identify the objects the signs depict, consult the full sign-list beginning on p. 129.

The proper value of each sign is the transliteration value given in the second column; the third column simply gives a way in which we, as English speakers, can vocalise these signs for our own convenience.

Most of these sounds resemble their English counterparts and can be transliterated directly into familiar letters from our own alphabet. However, some 1-consonant signs are used to represent sounds not present in spoken or written English, and these require specially adapted transliteration symbols of their own:

𓄿	*ꜣ*	glottal stop, like Cockney 'bo'le' for 'bottle'
𓇋	*ỉ*	Like the weak *y* sound at the end of 'tea'. Not to be confused with the vowel 'i'
𓂝	*ꜥ*	like trying to say 'ah' while swallowing
𓎛	*ḥ*	emphatic h, made in the throat
𓐍	*ḫ*	like Scottish 'loch'
𓄡	*ẖ*	like German 'ich'
𓈙	*š*	as in 'ship'
𓈎	*ḳ*	back k, made further back in the mouth
𓍿	*ṯ*	like 'tune'
𓆓	*ḏ*	like French 'dieu' or English 'joke'

Each 1-consonant sign represents a distinct sound in the ancient Egyptian language and so each needs its own transliteration symbol. It is important to include all the various dots and dashes when transliterating – they are not optional. In transliteration you should use the proper symbol given in the *second* column of the table on p. 3. This is true even if we find it difficult to tell the difference between two sounds. For example, *ḳ* and *k* are quite different sounds in Egyptian, even though distinguishing between them is rather difficult for us as English speakers.

There is no need to try and pronounce ancient Egyptian words exactly (in any case this is impossible, since the vowels are not written out for us). However, it is useful to be able to read out your transliterations and vocalise whole words, rather than spelling them out sign by sign. So, a purely conventional pronunciation, entirely for our convenience, is usually adopted. These are the renderings given in the third column in the table on p. 3. Many signs have values similar to letters of our own alphabet and present no problem, whereas the more unusual ones are usually given a convenient English approximation. We also need to add vowels. The convention normally adopted is to insert an 'e' between each consonant, except in the cases of *ꜣ* and *ꜥ*, where 'a' is used, and *w*, where 'u' is sometimes used because they are easier to pronounce. Once again, these pronunciations are purely a practical convenience and are not intended to bear any relation to spoken Egyptian. For example, the following is the word for 'birds', *ꜣpdw* (a writing discussed in §8), given with its transliteration and its English meaning:

 *ꜣpdw* birds

Purely for our own convenience we could pronounce this 'apedu'.

§5 Arrangement of signs

It may already have struck you, from looking at the examples discussed so far, that hieroglyphs are not arranged one after the other as in our own alphabetic system, but in balanced groups or 'blocks' arranged to fill the available space. In particular, some signs are placed over others in order to fill the space in a more pleasing manner. As an example, here is the name of the official Senbi (*snbỉ*) from Exercise 1.8 on p. 13:

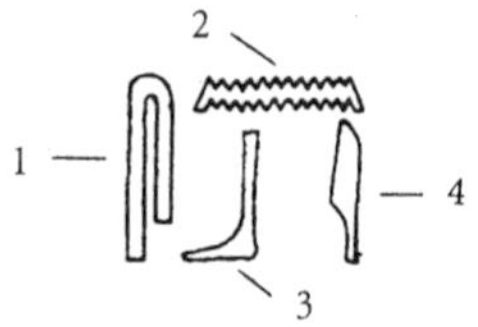

The name is written from left to right, starting with the *s* (1). But notice that the signs making up the name are grouped together, so that the *n* (2), as a long thin sign, is placed above both the tall thin signs for *b* (3) and *ỉ* (4), forming a block. The rule for such arrangements is quite simple: when you meet a block of hieroglyphs, read the top one(s) before the bottom one(s)

and then carry on as normal. You will see a number of examples of grouping throughout the rest of this chapter. You may wish to read this paragraph again when reading §7 on the direction of writing.

At this point, you may wish to attempt Exercises 1.1 and 1.2 on pp. 10-11.

§6 Determinatives: meaning-signs

So far we have studied words written out with sound-signs alone. However, in hieroglyphic writing words are sometimes written with meaning-signs, or *determinatives*, placed at the end of the word after the sound-signs. The following are examples of some common determinatives and words written with them:

	man and his occupations		*s*	man
	god, king		*skr*	(the god) Soker
	sun, light, time		*hrw*	day
	motion		*h3b*	send
	small bird used for bad, weak or little things		*bin*	bad, evil
	town, village		*ḳis*	Qis (place-name)

Determinatives do not contribute to the sounds of the word and so are not transliterated. From our point of view, they simply help us to get some general idea of the meaning of a word. A large number of signs can be used as determinatives, but for two reasons this fact should not get in your way. First, as already mentioned, we do not transliterate determinatives, so they do not need to be at the centre of your attention, especially early on in your studies. Secondly, in the inscriptions you will be reading in this book determinatives are quite frequently omitted. However, if you are bothered by a particular determinative, consult the full sign-list beginning on p. 129.

Two other common determinatives require a little more description.  (not to be confused with 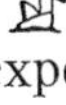 'man') is the meaning-sign used with words for what can be taken in or expelled through the mouth, either literally (eating, speaking) or metaphorically (emotions, attitudes, thinking) as well as the relevant activities connected with these, for example:

 *nis* call out, summon

The most common determinative, however, is 𓏛, the papyrus roll, used for abstract words or concepts. Although such words could not easily be represented by a picture, they could be written down, for example on papyrus, thus acquiring a tangible physical form. This written form could then be depicted in the shape of the rolled-up papyrus sheet:

 *snb* health, healthy

 *sḫr* counsel, plan, conduct, manner

One important word often written with the papyrus roll determinative is:

 *ḫt* thing(s)

The word *ḫt* is often written with the plural strokes 𓏪 (see §8 below), although it is not itself a plural word. Notice that, for reasons of spacing, the papyrus roll can be positioned either horizontally or vertically – you will find that a number of long thin signs can be arranged like this.

Sometimes a word can have more than one determinative:

 *nḏs* individual, ordinary man, person (from root meaning 'little, small')

Having a determinative thus gives us a second way of getting at a word – a general clue as to its meaning. This has the advantage that we can distinguish between two words written with the same sound-signs:

 *ỉꜣw* old, the old  *ỉꜣw* adoration, praise

As we shall see in Chapter 2, there are other features of the hieroglyphic script which tend to ensure that different words are written differently even when they share the same sounds.

In practice, however, as on the monumental inscriptions we shall be studying in this book, determinatives are often omitted. For example, in Exercise 1.2 you are asked to transliterate the following words (from the roasting scene in §1) without determinatives. They are shown here alongside examples with a determinative:

 or  roast  or  goose

At this point, you may wish to attempt Exercise 1.3 on p. 11.

§7 Direction of writing

So far, we have ordered the hieroglyphs following our own system of writing, i.e. writing them in lines from left to right. However, hieroglyphs were used in a more decorative manner than letters in our writing system; in particular, they often formed a fundamental part of the aesthetic scheme of a monument. Although we shall continue to present the hieroglyphs in left-to-right order within the text of this book, when you study real examples of inscriptions, these may well be organised from right to left (this is in fact the more usual direction) and possibly in columns. Fortunately, there is a very simple trick to reading hieroglyphs in the right order:

Read into the front or faces of the various signs, and from above to below.

Put another way, signs normally look towards the beginning of the text.

So, if we look at the following scene, the hieroglyphs are to be read in the order numbered. Notice that the orientation of a figure helps, particularly when there are not many signs with a clear 'front':

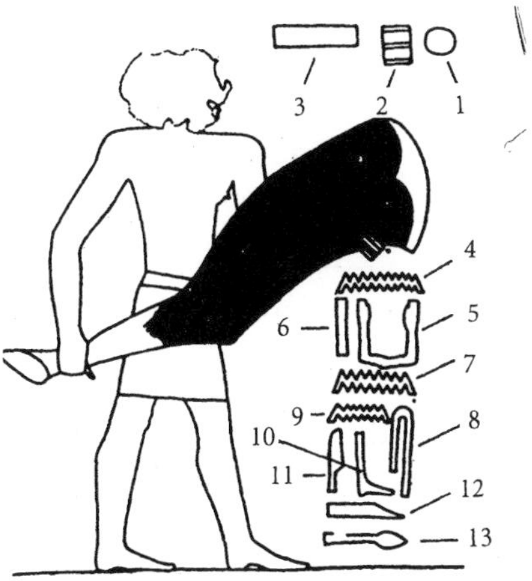

Offering scene from the tomb of Senbi at Meir (read from right to left) (Meir I, pl. 9)

In this case, the inscription is fitted into the space surrounding the figure. The overall direction of writing is indicated best by the foot-sign (10): to read into the front of this sign we need to read from right to left, the direction we would also need to look into the face of the accompanying figure. Vertically, we always read from top to bottom (see §5 above), so the text begins at the top right. The first three signs read horizontally above the top of the foreleg of beef carried by the figure. The remaining signs then read down the column, but still from right to left within each block, as indicated by nos 4-13. You may well recognise the name of Senbi discussed in §5 above. Compare the right-to-left writing of this name (nos 8-11) with the left-to-right ordering given in §5 (taken from another inscription in Senbi's tomb). To increase your confidence in this skill, a full vocabulary for this inscription is provided at the end of this chapter, so that you can practise reading it for yourself.

As an example reading from left to right, we can look once more at the inscription we used to introduce this book, shown on p. 8 with the order of the signs of the first line.

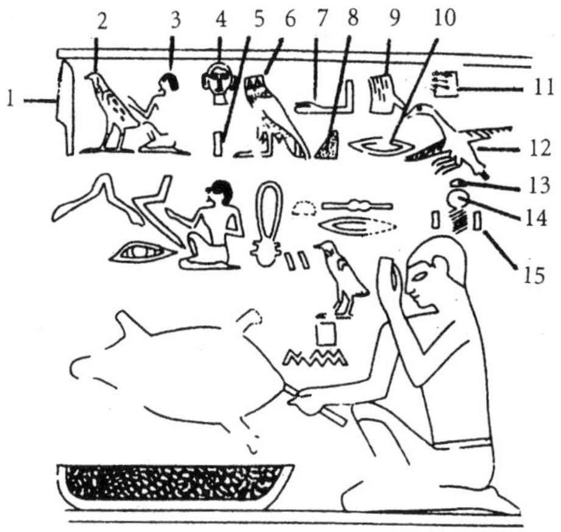

In this example, there are two rows of inscriptions, an upper one which is read first and a lower one, read second. Notice, once again, that the hieroglyphs have been fitted around the figure. So, Line 1 reads from left to right horizontally (reading into the face of the chick, the seated man, the owl and the bird in flight) and then at the end turns the corner, as it were, dropping down to finish in a column with nos 13-15. As with our writing system, we then return to the start of the next line and read along once more (into the face of signs such as the seated man and the chick).

As these examples also indicate, hieroglyphic signs were placed in a continuous sequence without any punctuation marks or word spacings. No doubt this will seem quite intimidating at first, but we hope to show you by example that, as you become familiar with the script and gain a grasp of useful words, this is nothing like as bad as it might seem. Exercise 1.8 (see pp. 13–14) will give you further practice in this skill.

§8 𓇋 *ỉ* and 𓅱 *w* and plurals

Hieroglyphic writing is quite economical. Along with vowels, the consonants 𓇋 *ỉ* and 𓅱 *w* are often omitted in writing, except at the beginning of words. This is particularly true for grammatical endings. For example, the plural is indicated by a *-w* ending (just as it is typically indicated in English by adding '-s', as in 'bird', 'birds'); this is sometimes fully written out, but more often the *-w* is omitted. The word for 'bird' (singular) is:

 *ȝpd* bird, fowl

For our convenience this word can be sounded 'aped'.

This is made plural by adding on a *-w*. A plural determinative of three strokes 𓏥 is also usually added. Since the determinative 𓏥 suffices to indicate the plural, the -*w* ending is often simply left out of the writing (and transliterated in brackets), leaving a more compact group of hieroglyphs:

 or  *ꜣpdw* or *ꜣpd(w)* birds

§9 Nouns

Learning to read hieroglyphs is, however, only one part of reading a hieroglyphic inscription, especially if you aspire to making real progress with your studies. Since hieroglyphs were used by the ancient Egyptians to write down their own language, it is necessary to build up a familiarity with how words are put together in Egyptian. Throughout this book, we will introduce you step by step to the most common features of ancient Egyptian which you are likely to meet in the sort of inscriptions studied here. Some of the ways Egyptian works are rather like English, and so will seem quite normal to you, but some of its features are not as we would expect from English, and will need a little more discussion and thought.

As a starting point, it is useful to know something about nouns in Egyptian (nouns are the words typically used to refer to people, objects, living things and the like). In Egyptian, all nouns are treated as being either masculine or feminine, even if there is no obvious reason (to us) why this should be the case; you may be familiar with a similar convention in French. Fortunately, this distinction is very easy to spot in ancient Egyptian, since feminine nouns almost always end in -*t*, whereas masculine nouns rarely do. For example:

 *s* man  *st* woman

Also there are no special words for 'the' or 'a' in classical Egyptian and so  *s* 'man' can mean either 'a man' or 'the man' (although one or the other often suggests itself in translation into English).

One feature of Egyptian which is rather like English is the use of prepositions (words which are 'pre-posed', or put before, others) to indicate locations ('in'), directions ('towards'), times ('during'), accompaniment ('with') and how things are done ('by'). As in English, the simplest prepositions tend to be very short words and are written with 1-consonant signs:

 *m* in, with, from, as

 n to(wards) (people), for

 r to(wards) (place), at

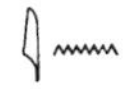 *in* by

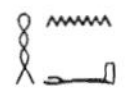 *ḥnꜥ* with

For example:

 *m pr* in the house

 *r pr* to the house

 *n snbi* for Senbi

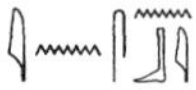 *in snbi* by Senbi

§10 Adjectives

An adjective is a word used to describe a noun, to give it a particular property or quality (e.g. 'a **stupid** man', 'a **clever** woman'). The distinctive feature about adjectives in Egyptian is that they *follow* their nouns and also they *agree* with the noun – if the noun is feminine and ends in *-t*, then so does the adjective:

 *s bin* the/an evil man

 *st bint* the/an evil woman

The word for 'this' behaves in a similar manner:

 *pn* this (masc.)

 *tn* this (fem.)

Like adjectives, *pn* and *tn* follow their noun and agree with it. An example of this occurs in the inscription used at the beginning of this book, where the text ends with the phrase 'this goose':

 *srw pn* this goose

Exercises

1.1 Kings' names

You are now in a position to read the names of several Old Kingdom kings. First, here is the name of the famous builder of the Great Pyramid of Giza, who is usually known by a Greek adaptation of his name as 'Cheops'. In hieroglyphs his name is written as follows (we have given you a conventional rendering in English afterwards to guide you in your transliteration; for the use of the name-ring or cartouche see p. 20):

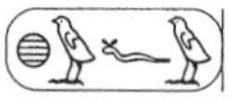 .... Khufu

Here are two further names of Old Kingdom kings. The first is one of two names of a 5th dynasty king, Djedkare Isesi. Which is given here? The second is a name shared by two kings of the 6th dynasty:

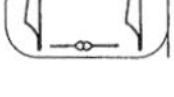 ....

 ....

1.2 Words from the roasting scene

In the roasting scene used in our introduction, some words are written out with 1-consonant signs. Transliterate the following and see if you can isolate the words in the original scene in §1:

 .... roast

 .... goose

1.3 Gods' names

The names of certain gods are typically written with 1-consonant signs. Transliterate the following. Once again, the traditional English rendering will help to guide you in most cases (although 'Anubis' is derived from a Greek version of the god's name – 'Inpu' or 'Anpu' might be a more conventional rendering into English). Remember to use the proper transliteration symbols from the second column in the table in §4. Any unfamilar sign (such as the seated dog) is a determinative and so not to be transliterated:

 .... Anubis

 .... Heket

 .... Ptah

 .... Sebek or Sobek

 .... Ra or Re

 .... Seker or Soker

'Sobek' and 'Soker' are usually rendered with an 'o' because of the Greek forms of these names. There is nothing of importance in this traditional practice.

Many readers of this book will be familiar with the famous pharaoh Akhenaten, his wife Nefertiti, and Akhenaten's innovative religious programme centred on the solar disc, the Aten. In hieroglyphs, the Aten is written as follows. Once again, try to transliterate:

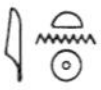 .... Aten

'Aten', like 'Anubis', shows the alternative conventional use of 'a' for initial *ỉ* ('Iten' would be the other way of pronouncing this word in English).

1.4 Transliterating words

Transliterate the following words written with 1-consonant signs and determinatives (any sign which is not a 1-consonant sign is a determinative and need not be transliterated):

 individual, ordinary man, person

 name

 festival

 bad, evil

 bird, fowl

 excellent, effective, astute

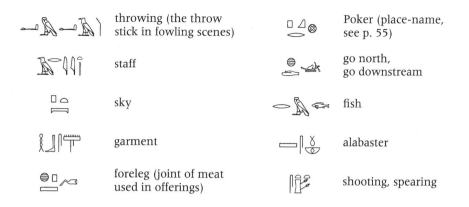

throwing (the throw stick in fowling scenes)	Poker (place-name, see p. 55)
staff	go north, go downstream
sky	fish
garment	alabaster
foreleg (joint of meat used in offerings)	shooting, spearing

1.5 Writing out words in hieroglyphs

Write out the following words in hieroglyphs using the determinative supplied. Remember to arrange the hieroglyphs into groups as noted in §5 above:

ḫr	fall		*ḫtm*	(v.) seal, close; (n.) a/the seal
sr	official		*ḳrst*	burial

1.6 Translation

Transliterate and translate the following phrases:

a   *b*

c   *d*

1.7 Translating the offering scene

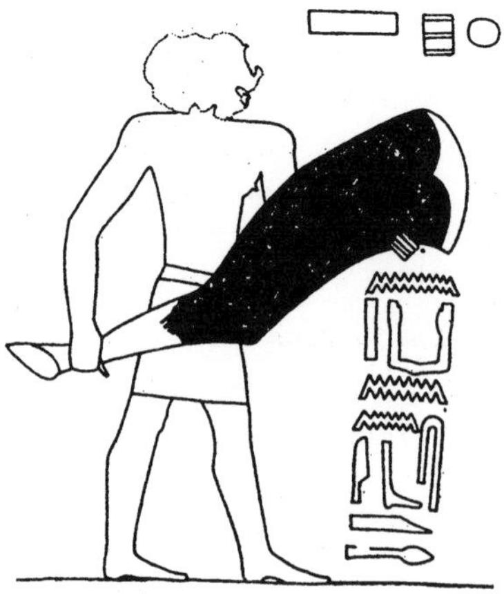

The scene on p. 12 was used to illustrate the use of hieroglyphs written in right-to-left order in §7 above. Have a go at translating the caption with the help of the vocabulary provided and the ordering of the signs given in §7. (The context of the scene is that the figure is offering the foreleg of a slaughtered bull to the tomb owner Senbi; the inscription relates his speech.) This exercise is useful in illustrating a couple of other points as well. First, these are drawings of real hieroglyphs found on the wall of the tomb of Senbi and not the standard hieroglyphs of a font such as that used in this book (recall how English written letters differ a little from standard type fonts). This is really just a matter of getting used to variability, particularly in the infill of signs – use the vocabulary provided to see the standard hieroglyphs. Secondly, the inscription contains words written in other ways than with 1-consonant signs which you will not be able to read through at present. Instead, use a 'cut-and-paste' approach, relying on us to isolate the correct groups of hieroglyphs in the vocabulary and to give their correct reading and meaning. You should just 'cut-and-paste' the relevant groups into your translations. By the end of the next chapter, even these words should be clear to you.

VOCABULARY

	*mꜣꜥ-ḫrw*	the justified		*n kꜣ n*	for the ka of
	*ḫpš*	foreleg (of ox used in offering)		*snbi*	Senbi (name)

(*mꜣꜥ-ḫrw* is used like our own R.I.P as a phrase referring to the blessed dead; offerings are made to the ka-spirit of the deceased.)

Note the interaction of art and text in this example, where the foreleg is an integral part of the scene, but also serves as the determinative of the word *ḫpš* (it can be 'read' at the correct point of the inscription at the end of the word for foreleg).

This inscription comes from the Middle Kingdom tombs at Meir, the cemetery site for Qis, the principal town of the 14th Upper Egyptian nome (province). We shall make use of these tombs, particularly that of the governor Senbi, for scenes to supplement your study of the Middle Kingdom stelae in the British Museum.

1.8 Study exercise: A fishing and fowling scene

Transliterate and translate the labels above the scene on p. 14 using the vocabulary and notes below the picture.

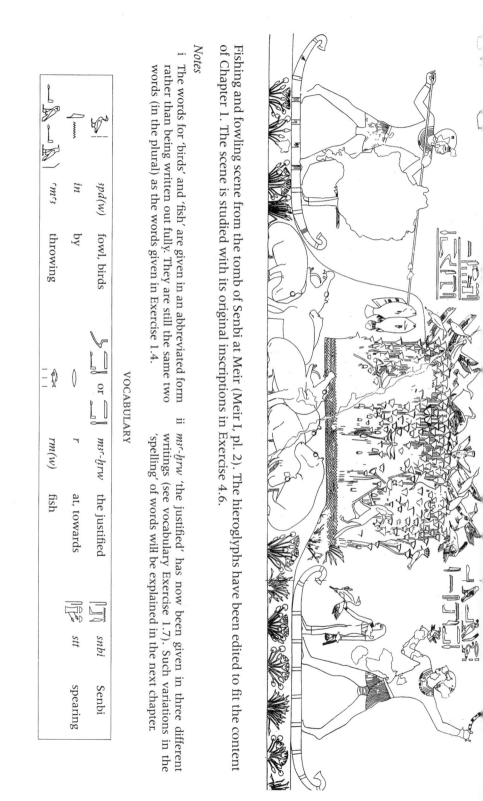

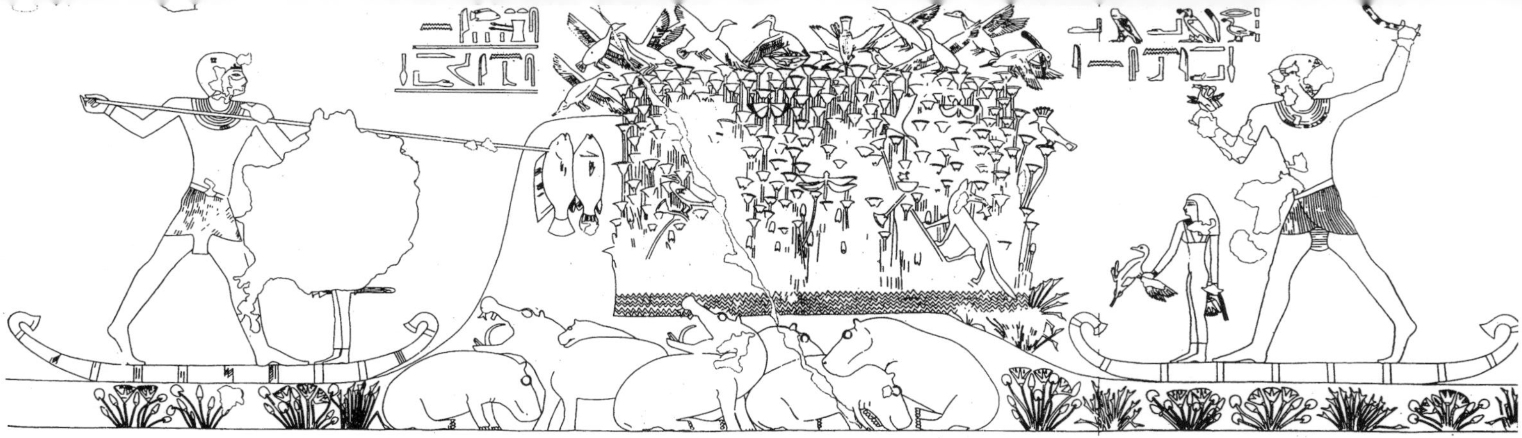

Fishing and fowling scene from the tomb of Senbi at Meir (Meir I, pl. 2). The hieroglyphs have been edited to fit the content of Chapter 1. The scene is studied with its original inscriptions in Exercise 4.6.

Notes

i The words for 'birds' and 'fish' are given in an abbreviated form rather than being written out fully. They are still the same two words (in the plural) as the words given in Exercise 1.4.

ii *mꜣꜥ-ḫrw* 'the justified' has now been given in three different writings (see vocabulary Exercise 1.7). Such variations in the 'spelling' of words will be explained in the next chapter.

VOCABULARY

	ꜣpd(w)	fowl, birds	or	*mꜣꜥ-ḫrw*	the justified		*snbi*	Senbi
	in	by		*r*	at, towards		*stt*	spearing
	ꜥmꜥꜣ	throwing		*rm(w)*	fish			

Chapter 2

More uses of hieroglyphs

The aim of this chapter is to introduce you to the 2-consonant and 3-consonant signs, which provide much of the subtlety and flexibility of the hieroglyphic script. It will also supply you with the information needed to read the names of various famous kings of ancient Egypt, including the names on the Abydos king-list in the British Museum.

§11 2-consonant signs

The second major group of signs are the 2-consonant signs, which contribute two consonants to the reading of a word. We have already seen an example in the use of the 2-consonant sign *pr* in the word *pr* 'go (out)'. The 2-consonant signs are rather common – over eighty are used in this book – and becoming familiar with them represents the major hurdle to be overcome in reading hieroglyphs. The sign-list on p. 128 gives a table of the most common 2-consonant signs used in the inscriptions studied, and we shall also introduce several at a time in the vocabularies to the various exercises to allow you to become familiar with them in convenient numbers. The following are some common examples of 2-consonant signs to get you started, along with some common words in which they occur (including *pr* again so that you can see how the table works):

SIGN	EXAMPLE		SIGN	EXAMPLE	
ꜥꜣ	*ꜥꜣ*	great, large	*bꜣ*	*bꜣk*	servant
wr	*wr*	great, important	*mr*	*mr*	love, want
nb	*nb*	lord	*pr*	*pr*	go out
ḥs	*ḥs*	praise, favour	*ḫꜣ*	*ḫꜣ*	thousand

Consider the word *bꜣk* 'servant'. In its most basic form, the word is built up through using the 2-consonant sign *bꜣ* followed by the 1-consonant sign *k*, which together give the reading of the word as *bꜣk* (it may also be finished off by a seated man determinative – see §6 above – showing us that the word refers to a person). Notice how this gives a more visually distinctive writing for the word than if it were simply written out with 1-consonant signs. Although we might view the number of 2-consonant signs as rather forbidding, it is nothing compared to the enormous number of words which any language contains. By having a mixed system in which they can be written with differing combinations of hieroglyphs, words take on more distinctive and memorable writings than if they were simply written out in an alphabet-like system (think of the difficulties of English spelling!).

The second noticeable point in the writing of some of these words is that 1-consonant signs often occur as *sound complements* fleshing out the reading of a 2-consonant sign, helping to jog the memory, as it were, about its reading. There is a simple rule about this: if a 1-consonant sign shares the same value as an accompanying 2-consonant sign, then this 1-consonant sign is not read as a separate sound. So, if we look at  again, we read *pr* and not *prr* even though it is written with  *pr* + *r*, because *r* jogs our memory about the *r* of *pr*.

If, however, the 1-consonant sign has a different value from the sounds of an accompanying 2-consonant sign, then it should be read as a separate sound. So, if we look at the word  *bꜣk*, then the 1-consonant sign  *k* must be read separately, since the sign  only reads *bꜣ* on its own. So read *bꜣk*.

From our point of view, this might seem an unnecessarily complex way to go about writing words, but there are a number of advantages. For example, such a system provides the flexibility to be able to write words in blocks as noted in §5. More importantly, it allows a good deal of flexibility in the actual choice of signs used; this was particularly useful in view of the fact that most hieroglyphic inscriptions were written on fixed and inflexible surfaces such as stone.

Suppose that we have two inscriptions, each with a different-sized space left at the end of a line, and we wish to write the word *bꜣk* 'servant' in each of these spaces. The hieroglyphic system allows us a convenient and elegant way out of our problem. In the smaller space we can write *bꜣk* as it is written in the table above: . In the larger space, we could include a sound-complement  fleshing out the *ꜣ* of the *bꜣ*-sign and thus fill the slightly larger space: .

The two words read just the same, they are just 'spelt out' slightly differently. Words in hieroglyphic writing, therefore, do not have one single correct spelling but are rather 'elastic' and can be contracted or expanded through, for example, the inclusion or omission of sound-complements. Fortunately, we can leave it to the ancient Egyptians to do all the spelling for us – the important point for us is just to be aware of the flexibility of the script and observe it in action.

§12 3-consonant signs

The final major group of sound-signs are the 3-consonant signs, which contribute three consonants to the reading of a word. 3-consonant signs are also often accompanied by one or two 1-consonant signs as sound complements helping to flesh out the reading of the sign. There are far fewer of these signs and also many of them are emblematic – they are used only in certain words and are often connected to, or come to be emblems for, the words in which they are used. Perhaps the most famous example of these signs is 𓋹 *ꜥnḫ*, 'ankh', used in the word for 'life':

SIGN		EXAMPLE			SIGN		EXAMPLE		
𓋹	*ꜥnḫ*	𓋹𓈖𓐍	*ꜥnḫ*	life	𓄊	*wsr*	𓄊𓋴𓂋	*wsr*	strong, powerful
𓄤	*nfr*	𓄤𓆑𓂋	*nfr*	perfect, good	𓊹	*nṯr*	𓊹𓏤	*nṯr*	god
𓊵	*ḥtp*	𓊵𓏏𓊪	*ḥtp*	rest, satisfy	𓆣	*ḫpr*	𓆣𓂋	*ḫpr*	become
𓐙	*mꜣꜥ*	𓐙𓂝𓆄	*mꜣꜥ*	true, right, proper	𓊤	*ḫrw*	𓊤𓅱𓀁	*ḫrw*	voice

The two words *mꜣꜥ* and *ḫrw* have already been met in the phrase *mꜣꜥ-ḫrw* 'true of voice' or 'justified'. This, as already noted, is a common epithet bestowed on the blessed dead (whose conduct has been judged before the gods to be true) and is used after the names of the deceased in a similar manner to our R.I.P. (𓌳 is a 2-consonant sign reading *mꜣ*):

𓌳𓐙𓂝𓐍𓊤𓀁 *mꜣꜥ-ḫrw* true of voice, justified

You have encountered this in more condensed writings. (See further §14 on p. 18 below.)

§13 Ideograms: sound-meaning signs

The final signs to be looked at in this chapter are the sound-meaning signs (ideograms) which combine sound and meaning and which come closest to our own preconceptions of how a picture-script should work:

𓄣𓏤	*ib*	heart	𓂋𓏤	*r*	mouth
𓂝𓏤	*ꜥ*	arm	𓇳𓏤	*rꜥ*	the sun
𓉐𓏤	*pr*	house	𓁷𓏤	*ḥr*	face

As the examples indicate, these signs are often followed by 𓏤 which helps to highlight the ideogram usage, as well as noting that only one 'heart' etc. is meant; it also serves as a space filler to give a convenient grouping of the signs. A fuller list of ideograms is given on pp. 128-129.

Sound-meaning signs can be accompanied by sound complements or determinatives:

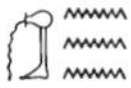	*wꜥb*	pure, priest		*rnpt*	year
	*sḏm*	hear		*tꜣ*	land

This usage of signs illustrates an important point for using this book. Although you may be able to 'spell out' a couple of the words given in this section, most of them will not be immediately readable (you should, however, rapidly grow used to reading  as *wꜥb*, for example). Therefore we encourage you to focus on words as a whole, rather than trying to puzzle through the use of every single sign from first principles. We will do the work for you by supplying you with words in the format used in the table above: hieroglyphic writing followed by transliteration and translation. If you concentrate on whole words as opposed to single signs, you should find that you make faster progress in reading.

§14 Variant writings

Hieroglyphs are written in groups, accommodating aesthetic considerations and the limits of physical space by using differing combinations of signs. For these reasons, words can be written in a number of different ways. For example, we have already encountered the phrase *mꜣꜥ-ḫrw* 'true of voice' or 'justified' in a number of different writings:

As already noted, we can safely leave it to the ancient Egyptians to show us how it should be done. We need only be aware that variant spelling is a perfectly normal feature of hieroglyphic writing.

However, it is worth noting that 'spelling' is constrained by convention and tradition within fairly strict limits. So, even though *mꜣꜥ-ḫrw* is written out in a number of different ways, there are usually distinctive and recognisable elements to the phrase (in this case and). Furthermore, by tradition, *mꜣꜥ* is never found written out with 1-consonant signs as *  *mꜣꜥ* (* is the symbol for 'not found'); rather the range of 'spelling' of *mꜣꜥ* concerns whether *mꜣꜥ* was written along with  *mꜣ* as a sound complement (often combined into ), and perhaps also with other sound complements in differing combinations, to suit aesthetic and physical considerations.

§15 Writing the plural (see also Reference table on p. 149)

The most common way of writing the plural has already been discussed in §8 above. It is typically written with plural strokes (ı ı ı) and may or may not show a *-w* sound-sign (in the latter case, a *w* is added to the transliteration in brackets for convenience):

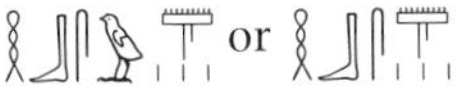 *ḥbsw* or *ḥbs(w)* clothes

Another way of writing the plural is for a sign to be repeated three times:

 *tꜣ(w)* lands

This method is rarer in practice, although it is favoured for certain words, such as *tꜣ(w)* 'lands'.

Egyptian also shows a restricted use of a dual ending: msc.  *-wy* and fem.  *-ty* (indicating two of something), but this is common only with things which tend to come in pairs:

 *ꜥwy* arms  *tꜣwy* the two lands (Egypt: Delta and Valley)

tꜣwy is written by repeating two signs, like the second plural method noted above.

§16 𓎟 *nb* 'all, every, any' and 𓎟 *nb* 'lord'

There are two important words which can be written alike. The first is the word for 'all', 'every' or 'any':

 nb all, every, any

𓎟 *nb* 'all, every, any', behaves rather like an adjective (see §10): it *follows* the noun it goes with and, like an adjective, agrees with it:

 *ḫt nbt* everything

𓎟 also occurs in another common word, the word *nb* meaning 'lord', which, in its most abbreviated form, is written simply:

 nb lord

Fortunately, when *nb* means 'lord' it comes first in expressions:

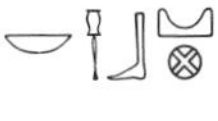 *nb ꜣbḏw* lord of Abydos

(See Exercise 2.2 for *ꜣbḏw* 'Abydos'.)

So the rule is quite simple: when *nb* comes second in its phrase (and agrees with the first noun) then it is the word *nb* 'all, every, any'; when it comes first in its phrase, it is the word *nb* 'lord'.

§17 Royal names and titles

One of the principal goals of this chapter is to equip you to read the names of the kings of Egypt. In the next few paragraphs, we will deal with some of the background about royal names, focusing on the titles, epithets and the dating formula. In the Exercises to this chapter, we shall set you loose on the names of the kings themselves.

The king in ancient Egypt had an elaborate titulary made up of his names, titles and epithets. From the Old Kingdom onwards, each king had five names, of which three are particularly common on monuments (the other two – the 'two ladies' and the 'golden Horus' names – are used less often). The three common names are the Horus name and the names contained in cartouches – the praenomen and the nomen.

The *Horus name* designates the king as the god Horus, the son and successor of Osiris (for whom, see pp. 40-42). The name is introduced by the falcon  *ḥr*. As an example the Horus name of Senwosret I is:

 *ḥr ꜥnḫ-mswt* the Horus Ankhmesut

The other two common names are written in cartouches (name-rings). The *praenomen*, or first cartouche-name (a name assigned on the king's accession), follows the  *nsw-bi͗ty* title 'king of the dualities', 'dual king' – i.e. the king as ruler of the dualities which composed the Egyptian world: Upper and Lower Egypt; desert and cultivation; the human and the divine. It has been traditional to focus on the division of Egypt into the Nile Valley and the Delta and to translate this title as 'king of Upper and Lower Egypt'. The praenomen of Senwosret I is:

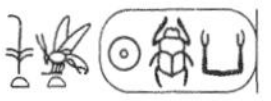 *nsw-bi͗ty ḫpr-kꜣ-rꜥ* the king of Upper and Lower Egypt Kheperkare

The *nomen*, or second cartouche-name, is the king's own birth name and might be common to other members of the dynasty. It is also the name by which scholars nowadays refer to the kings: hence we have Senwosret I, II, and III in the 12th dynasty. The numbers are a modern convention and do not occur in the ancient names. The nomen is typically introduced by the  *sꜣ rꜥ* title 'son of Re' – i.e. the king as the heir of the sun-god Re on earth. The nomen of Senwosret I is:

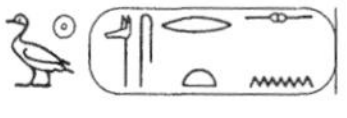 *sꜣ rꜥ s-n-wsrt* son of Re Senwosret

(See Exercise 2.7 on pp. 26-27 for the readings of the cartouche names themselves, and the ordering of the signs.)

A couple of other titles of the king (typically accompanying the praenomen) are:

 *nṯr nfr* the perfect god

 *nb tꜣwy* lord of the two lands

§18 Royal epithets

The king's name and titles are usually associated with a number of epithets. Among the most common are epithets connected with life:

 *ꜥnḫ ḏt* living enduringly

 *di͗ ꜥnḫ* given life

often extended:

 *mi͗ rꜥ* like Re

 *ḏt r nḥḥ* enduringly and repeatedly (for ever and eternity)

On the written order of the phrase *mi͗ rꜥ* 'like Re', you may wish to look ahead to §22 in the next chapter.

§19 Dating

Dates were recorded in ancient Egypt according to the regnal year of the reigning king and not by some absolute dating system like BC/AD. The dating formula has a fixed and regular form based around the following words, along with the names, titles and epithets of the king and the number of years of his reign:

 *rnpt-sp* regnal year

 *ḫr* under

 *ḥm* person

 n of

ḥm is used to refer indirectly to the king.

Egyptian numbering is decimal, broken up into tens and units. The tens are reckoned by repetition of the sign ∩ (so ∩∩∩ = 30) and the units by repetition of I (so IIII = 4). Consider the following example (here year 28 of king Nimaatre Amenemhet III) which shows how the formula is put together and how the numbering system works:

The date in the lunette of BM EA 827:

BM EA 827: *rnpt-sp 28 ḫr ḥm n nsw-bi͗ty (n)-mꜣꜥt-rꜥ ꜥnḫ ḏt*
Regnal year 28 under the person of the king of Upper and Lower Egypt Nimaatre living enduringly

(On the title and epithets of the king, see the previous paragraphs. On the cartouche name of the king himself, see Exercise 2.7 on pp. 26-27. The *n* of Nimaatre was omitted in the original.)

Excursus: chart of royal dynasties

Kings of Egypt prior to the invasion by Alexander the Great(332 BC) are organised by scholars into thirty dynasties, further arranged into major periods known as Kingdoms (normally when only one king at a time ruled Egypt) and Intermediate Periods (when the kingship was often divided). This book principally concerns monuments from the First Intermediate Period and Middle Kingdom (*c.*2150 BC–*c.*1641 BC), but the kings listed below are discussed on pp. 26-31.

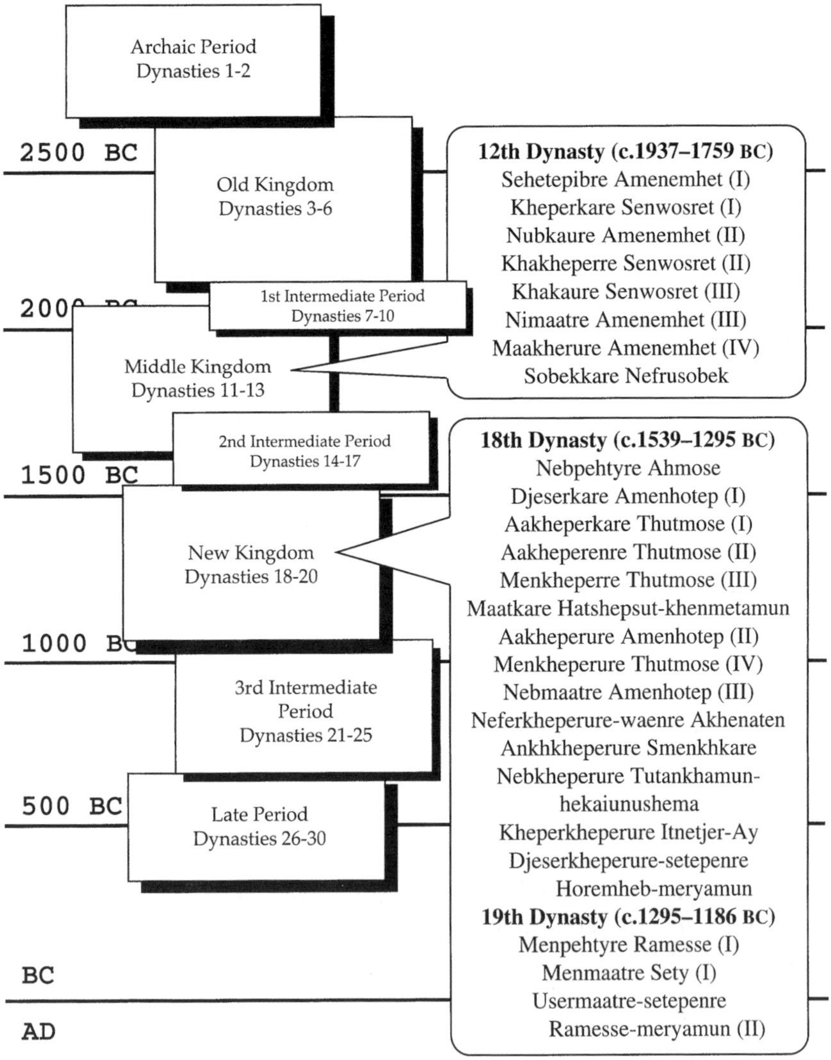

Note: all dates are approximate; you will find slightly different schemes used in different books.

Exercises

2.1 Signs

The following are a list of signs to be used in the Exercises. They are worth memorising (writing them out is a good way of familiarising yourself with them).

a. 2-consonant signs

Some of these sign occur in the word exercises below; others will be of use when studying kings' names in Exercises 2.7 and 2.8:

	ꜣb or *mr*		*wp*		*mr*		*nb*		*kꜣ*
or	*ꜥꜣ*		*mꜣ*		*mr*		*ḥꜥ*		*dw*
	wꜣ		*mn*		*ms*		*sꜣ*		*ḏd*

b. 3-consonant signs

The following 3-consonant signs were introduced in the main text above. Write out and learn these signs and the following common words they occur in, using the opportunity to follow the use of sound-complements and determinatives.

	ꜥnḫ		*ꜥnḫ*	life		*wsr*		*wsr*	powerful
	nfr		*nfr*	good		*nṯr*		*nṯr*	god
	ḥtp		*ḥtp*	rest, satisfy		*ḫpr*		*ḫpr*	become

A further useful 3-consonant sign is: *ẖnm*

c. Ideograms

	SIGN		EXAMPLE	
	A55, vase with water flowing, combined with leg		*wꜥb*	pure
	C9, flat alluvial land with grains of sand		*tꜣ*	land
	F42, road bordered by shrubs		*wꜣt*	road, way

To aid you in further study, these signs have been quoted with their classification (composed of a letter and a number) as found in the sign-list on pp. 129–143.

Note: often occurs without the grains of sand as (C10) alone.

2.2 Words

a. Copy out and transliterate the following words (you may wish to refer to the list of signs above or the sign-tables at the end of the book):

 .... son

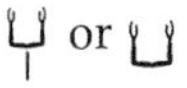 .... ka (the spirit of sustenance)

Since both of these common words rely on a single 2-consonant sign, it is not at all unusual to find them written at their briefest with just the 2-consonant sign.

 .... road, way

 .... love, wish, want, desire

 .... companion

 .... open, separate

(Notice that in the word for 'road', 'way',  can be used as a determinative with the word 'spelt out', or as an ideogram as in Exercise 2.1.)

b. Two important town-sites which occur in common epithets of the god Osiris are:

 .... Abydos

 .... Djedu (Busiris)

c. Some more names of gods:

 .... Amun

 .... Khnum

Try and transliterate the name of the god Wepwawet (you may need to consult §15 again):

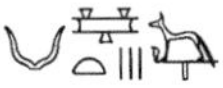 .... Wepwawet

The names of these gods can be written with or without the determinative for gods:  (A3).

2.3 Variant writings

In §14 in the text, you were introduced to the notion of variant writings, which allow a word to be stretched or compressed to fit space. The example used was the phrase *mꜣꜥ-ḫrw* 'justified' or 'true of voice', used as an epithet of the blessed dead. The variants given in previous examples are repeated here. Work through the writings, identifying the various signs, and satisfying yourself that despite the differences, they all yield the same transliteration: *mꜣꜥ-ḫrw*.

2.4 Expressions

Transliterate and translate the following phrases (both of which are common elements of the offering formula which you will study in more depth in Chapter 3):

a.  *b.* 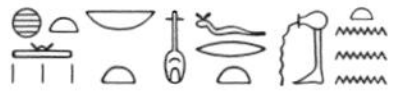

As so often, the same phrase can be written in a more condensed manner (although it is read in the same way), for example:

In this case the feminine ending –*t* has been omitted in writing from *nbt, nfrt* and *wꜥbt*. The feminine ending is often left out when abbreviating common words or phrases. (You may wish to consult §§9 and 10 on nouns and adjectives in Egyptian.)

2.5 Words

Some very common words are written with otherwise uncommon signs and with some idiosyncracies of their own. Copy out the following and read the accompanying notes:

 or 	*ỉt*	father	It seems that  is an obscure determinative here; however, the common phrase *ỉt=f* 'his father' is probably influential too (cf. §§33, 36).
 or 	*ꜣsir*	Osiris	Written with E60-seat above A36-eye for reasons which are still obscure. *ꜣsir* is a recently suggested reading (rather than older *wsir*)
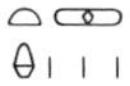	*t*	bread	Written with D25 and F9 or F10-bread determinatives and plural strokes. In offering formulae it is often abbreviated to .

2.6 Dating

The following are examples of dates from British Museum stelae. It is perhaps better to do this exercise after the study exercises on pp. 26-30, when you will be able to read the kings' names more easily.

The lunette of the round-topped stela of Senwosretsenbu (BM EA 557) begins:

BM EA 557: 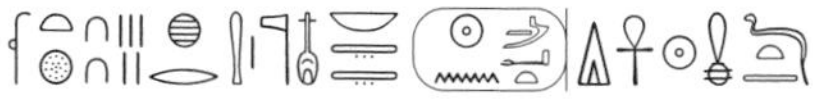

The word *n* 'of' has been omitted after *ḥm*.

In the first line of BM EA 586 the king's cartouche is surmounted by the sky hieroglyph, which is not read:

BM EA 586, Line 1: 

BM EA 567 begins with a date; the writing of nsw-bỉty is to fit the rounded shape:

BM EA 567,
Lines 1-2:

2.7 Study exercise: Middle Kingdom kings of the 12th dynasty

It is now time for you to read through the cartouche names of various kings of Egypt. The kings we have selected come from the some of the most celebrated dynasties of ancient Egypt: the 12th dynasty in the Middle Kingdom, and the 18th, 19th and 20th dynasties in the New Kingdom. You can either piece their names together from the sign resources provided below or you can go further and refer back to Chapters 1 and 2 (as well as making use of the sign-tables at the end of the book) to improve your familiarity with the signs.

The two most common names of the king – the praenomen and nomen – are written in cartouches and are thus easy to spot. However, the way that the names themselves are written is actually surprisingly complex, playing with the various resources of the script for aesthetic and spacing reasons. The one factor we have not covered so far (because it finds a more appropriate place in Chapter 3) is that elements drawing on divine names are written first, regardless of the order in which they are read. For example, the sun-disc *rꜥ* (the name of the sun god) regularly appears first in the praenomen but is read last (as the transliteration values and Anglicisation of the names below show). For the purposes of this exercise, we would ask you to follow the reading order we give below, but you may wish to look forward to §22 in Chapter 3 for an account of this peculiarity.

Fill in the first cartouche names from the list below into the proper place in the following table (the first one is done for you). Notice, once again, that the element *rꜥ* is written before the other elements of the name (similarly with *wsrt* in *s-n-wsrt*), although it is not read first:

Sehetepibre *sḥtp-ỉb-rꜥ*
Amenemhet (I) *ỉmn-m-ḥꜣt*

....
Senwosret (I) *s-n-wsrt*

....
Amenemhet (II) *ỉmn-m-ḥꜣt*

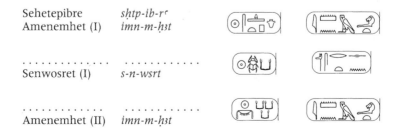

....
Senwosret (II) *s-n-wsrt* 

....
Senwosret (III) *s-n-wsrt* 

....
Amenemhet (III) *imn-m-ḥ3t* 

....
Amenemhet (IV) *imn-m-ḥ3t* 

....
Nefrusobek *nfrw-sbk* 

List of first-cartouche names (in jumbled order):

ḫʿ-k3w-rʿ Khakaure	*ḫʿ-ḫpr-rʿ* Khakheperre	*ḫpr-k3-rʿ* Kheperkare	*m3ʿ-ḫrw-rʿ* Maakherure
n-m3ʿt-rʿ Nimaatre	*nbw-k3w-rʿ* Nubkaure	*sḥtp-ib-rʿ* Sehetepibre	*sbk-k3-rʿ* Sobekkare

SIGNS

	*ib*	*ib* heart		*imn*	*amun/amen-* (the god) Amun
	*wsrt*	*wosret* the powerful one		*m*	*em* in
	*m3ʿ*	*maa* true		*m3ʿt*	*maat* (the goddess) Maat (truth)
	n	*en* or *ni* of		*nbw*	*nub* gold
	*nfrw*	*nefru* beauty		*ḥ3t*	*het/hat* (fore)front
	*ḫʿ*	*kha* appear(ance)		*ḫpr*	*kheper* being/form
	*ḫrw*	*kheru* voice		*s*	*s(e)* man
 or 	*sbk*	*sebek/sobek* (the god) Sobek		*sḥtp*	*sehetep* make satisifed
	*k3*	*ka* the ka-spirit		*k3w*	*kau* the ka-spirits

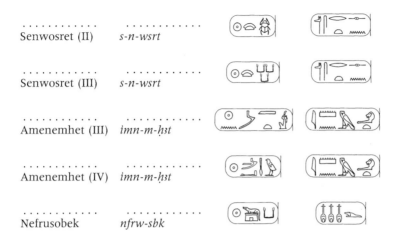

All the first cartouche names contain the following element:

⊙ *rꜥ* — *ra* or *re*
(the god) Re (or Ra)

Many of these elements have proper meaning as words on their own, which we indicate here. However, there is no need to try and translate the names.

2.8 Study exercise: New Kingdom kings

Transliterate both the cartouche names for each of the following New Kingdom kings, using the aids provided. A complicating factor is that, during the New Kingdom, it is not at all uncommon to find epithets included within royal cartouches. Some of the names below contain such epithets (for example that of the ruling queen Hatshepsut, which regularly includes the epithet *ḫnmt-imn* – 'joined with (the god) Amun'). If the epithet contains the name of a god, this divine element may be written at the front of the cartouche, even if it is not read first. Follow the lead given in the Anglicised versions of the names below:

Nebpehtyre
Ahmose

Djeserkare
Amenhotep (I)

Aakheperkare
Thutmose (I)

Aakheperenre
Thutmose (II)

Maatkare
Hatshepsut-khenmetamun

Menkheperre
Thutmose (III)

Aakheperure
Amenhotep hekaiunu (II)

Menkheperure
Thutmose (IV)

Nebmaatre
Amenhotep hekawaset (III)

Neferkheprure-waenre
Akhenaten

Nebkheperure
Tutankhamen-hekaiunushema

Djeserkheperure-setepenre
Horemheb-meryamun

Menpehtyre Ramesse (I)	
Menmaatre Sety-meryenptah (I)	
Usermaatre-setepenre Ramesse-meryamun (II)	
Usermaatre-meryamun Ramesse-hekaiunu (III)	

VOCABULARY

	*ꜣḫ*	*akh* spirit		*ỉꜥḥ*	*(i)ah* moon-god
	*ỉwnw*	*iunu* Heliopolis	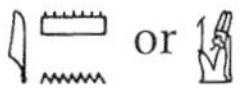	*ỉmn*	*amun/amen-* (the god) Amun
	*ỉtn*	*aten* Aten (solar disc)	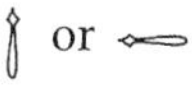	*ꜥꜣ*	*aa* great
	*ꜥnḫ*	*ankh* life/living		*wꜥ*	*wa* the (sole) one
	*wꜣst*	*waset* Thebes (place-name)		*wsr*	*weser/user* powerful
	*pḥtt* for *pḥty*	*pehty* strength		*ptḥ*	*ptah* (the god) Ptah
	m	*em* in		*mꜣꜥt*	*maat* Maat (truth)
	*mn*	*men* established		*mry*	*mery* beloved
	*ms*	*mose* bear, form		*n*	*en* of
	*nb*	*neb* lord		*nfr*	*nefer* perfect
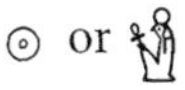	*rꜥ*	*re/ra* (the god) Re		*ḥꜣt*	*hat* front, first
	*ḥb*	*heb* festival		*ḥr*	*hor* (the god) Horus
	*ḥḳꜣ*	*heka* ruler	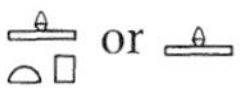	*ḥtp*	*hetep/ hotep* satisfied
	*ḫpr*	*kheper* being/form		*ḫprw*	*kheperu* beings/forms
	*ḫnmt*	*khenmet* joined (with)	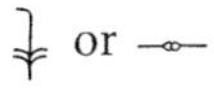	*sw,* *s(w)*	*su, se* him

VOCABULARY (CONTINUED)

	*sty*	*Sety* Sety, i.e. man of (the god) Seth		*stp*	*setep* chosen
	*špswt*	*shepsut* distinguished women		*šmꜥ*	*shema* southern
	*kꜣ*	*ka* the ka-spirit		*twt*	*tut* image
	*ḏḥwty*	*Thut-* (the god) Thoth		*ḏsr*	*djeser* sacred/holy

2.9 Study exercise: BM EA 117 (the Abydos king-list of Ramesses II)

The 'king-list' of Ramesses II shown on p. 31 originally came from his temple at Abydos. Modelled on a similar list in his father Seti I's mortuary temple nearby, the list forms part of an elaborate offering formula (*ḥtp-di-nsw*; see Chapter 3) for the cult of previous kings. Originally, there were 78 cartouches in the upper registers (the 76 found in the Seti I list plus the two cartouche names of Ramesses II). This number probably reflects cultic tradition, the space available on the wall, and possibly the 76 forms of the sun-god enumerated in the religious text known as the Litany of Re. The kings are identified by praenomen beneath which are determinatives of seated kings alternately wearing the white  and red  crowns. The names of Ramesses II (alternating between nomen and praenomen) are repeated in the bottom register and show a range of variant writings for the nomen. Reconstructing the top line from the Seti I king-list, the overall format is as follows:

[An offering which the king gives before Ptah-Sokar-Osiris ... a thousand bread and beer, etc.] to king X as a gift of Ramesses II:

	*n nsw*	for the king
	*m dd*	as a gift of (literally, in the giving of)

The word *nsw* is written using  which is also a variant for common in the New Kingdom (compare the more usual spelling of *nsw* in §23).

The king-list shows some interesting gaps between the Middle and New Kingdom (between the fourth and fifth cartouches of the second surviving register) and within the 18th dynasty. Use the royal names listed in the previous Exercises and the chart of royal dynasties on p. 22 to identify the missing kings and dynasties for yourself.

Chapter 3

Special writings

In this chapter we introduce you to a number of special writings: abbreviations, changes in the order of signs and defective writings. Since all of these are rather common, particularly in the rendering of titles and epithets, a knowledge of them is essential for successful monument reading in a museum. You are also introduced to the offering formula, probably the most common form of hieroglyphic inscription to be found on funerary monuments surviving from ancient Egypt. This chapter should also serve as a convenient reference resource to which you can return when studying various monuments later on in the book.

§20 Abbreviations

Abbreviated writings are common in the writing of titles and epithets:

 *ḥꜣty-ꜥ* governor, mayor  *ẖry-ḥbt* lector priest

ḥꜣty-ꜥ (literally, 'foremost of position') is written with the ideogram  *ḥꜣt* (front part of lion) over  *ꜥ* (arm); *ẖry-ḥbt* (literally, 'the carrier of the book of ritual') is written with abbreviated writings of both *ẖry* and *ḥbt* (without sound complements or determinatives). There is also graphic transposition, with the two tall signs placed either side of  *ẖr(y)* (see §21 below). Clearly such writings cannot be read sign by sign with any ease. Even after more than a century and a half of study, the exact reading of some words remains contentious among Egyptologists! Hence we strongly recommend that you follow our general advice of concentrating on whole words rather than getting bogged down in the study of individual signs.

As we have already seen, abbreviated writings of the epithet usually bestowed on the blessed dead are common:

 *mꜣꜥ-ẖrw* written in full as:  true of voice, justified

§21 Change of order: spacing

The second feature is the switching of the order of signs to enable them to fit into the available space in a more satisfactory manner (termed more formally *graphic transposition*):

 instead of  *ḏdw* Djedu

BM EA 117 (The Abydos king-list of Ramesses II)
(carved and painted limestone; H. 135cm)

Graphic transposition also occurs in vertical columns:

 *ḏdw* Djedu, instead of 

Sometimes graphic transposition is a regular feature of the writing of a word:

 *mꜣꜣ* see, look at

This is regularly written with the determinative placed under the 2-consonant sign  *mꜣ*.

§22 Change of order: prestige

For reasons of prestige, names for gods and kings and related words sometimes precede closely connected words, although they are actually read afterwards (this is termed more formally *honorific transposition*). Honorific transposition is particularly common in epithets and titles:

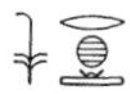	*rḫ nsw*	king's advisor, royal intimate		*ḥm-nṯr*	servant of the god, priest
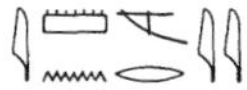	*mry ỉmn*	beloved of Amun		*mỉ rʿ*	like Re

(Notice that abbreviated writings are also common.)

You have already encountered this phenomenon in the writing of royal names in Exercises 2.7 and 2.8. A rather dramatic illustration of this point is the following writing of the nomen of Ramesses II (Ramesse-meryamun, 'Ramesses beloved of Amun'):

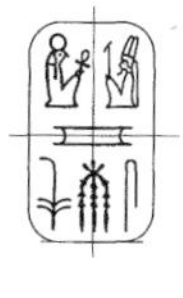

Here the two divine elements (Ra of the name Ramesses and Amun of the epithet 'beloved of Amun') have been written as seated gods and placed at the top of the cartouche facing each other, creating a vertical division. The low flat sign of *mr(y)* ('beloved') has been placed in the middle of the cartouche, creating a horizontal division. The vertical division is mirrored in the bottom half of the cartouche (giving the *ms-sw* or 'messe' part of Ramesses) where the three-pronged *ms*-sign stands in the centre between two tall thin signs (the *sw* and the *s*) both of which bend away at the top from the central *ms*-sign.

§23 Defective or strange writings

A few common words are written without the full set of sound-signs, probably for reasons of grouping; *nsw* 'king' is written in an unusual manner:

	*r(m)ṯ*	people		*ḥ(n)ḳt*	beer
	*s(my)t*	desert		*nsw*	king

§24 Titles

Office-holding played a central role in the élite culture of ancient Egypt, locating the individual within society, most notably in relation to the king (see also pp. 101-104). Titles come in two forms: official or administrative titles and conventional titles connected with status and authority. Abbreviated writings are common to both.

a. Conventional titles of status and authority

The two most common conventional titles are:

	*ḫtmty bỉty*	seal-bearer of the king	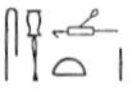	*smr wꜥt(y)*	sole companion

(The reading of *ḫtmty-bỉty* is unsure: other possibilities are *ḫtmw-bỉty* and *sḏꜣwty-bỉty;* for *bỉty* 'king', see p. 102.) These two titles often occur together.

b. Titles of office

Titles of office can be divided into secular and religious titles:

Secular titles

	*ḥꜣty-ꜥ*	governor, mayor		*m-r ꜥẖnwty*	overseer of the chamber

A number of titles are composed with the element  *m-r* (fully *ỉmy-r*) 'overseer':

	*m-r pr*	steward, overseer of the estate		*m-r mšꜥ*	overseer of the army

m-r probably means literally 'the one in whom is the word' (i.e. the one who has the authority to issue orders). On the basis of a graphic pun around *r* (which means both 'mouth' and 'word'), it is occasionally written with B44 tongue (the tongue being 'the one in the mouth'):

	*m-r pr*	steward

Religious titles

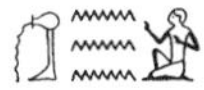	*wꜥb*	priest (literally, pure one)		*ḥm-nṯr*	priest (literally, servant of the god)
	*ḥry-sštꜣ*	master of secrets		*ḫry-ḥbt*	lector priest

It is not at all uncommon for titles to be written without determinatives.

§25 Epithets

Egyptian texts abound with epithets of gods, kings and officials. Here are a couple of related epithets particularly common on stelae:

 or  or 	*imꜣḫy* or *imꜣḫw*	venerable one, revered one, honourable one
	*nb imꜣḫ*	possessor of veneration/reverence

and other variants based on the fuller writings such as:  'reverence', 'veneration'.

These epithets are primarily applied to the blessed dead. After a life of official duty and ethical behaviour, the blessed dead were revered by the living (who perpetuate their memory on earth, particularly through offerings) and honoured before the gods (with whom they exist beyond death as transfigured spirits). The latter is often expressed in the following way:

	*imꜣḫy ḫr ꜣsir*	the revered one before Osiris

§26 The offering formula

Formulae comprise relatively fixed combinations of words and so can be read without a detailed understanding of their internal grammar. The most common example, the offering formula, is a ubiquitous feature of the hieroglyphic monuments found in museums throughout the world. By working through, and becoming familiar with, the elements of the formula discussed below, you will gain access to a vast number of hieroglyphic inscriptions.

The offering formula merges two related functions: official and personal. In official terms, the status of the deceased as one of the blessed dead was linked to the successful performance of official functions in royal service and ethical behaviour in life. This success was instrumental in qualifying the deceased for access to the means of commemoration in terms of memorial inscriptions and funerary monuments. One purpose of the offering formula was to allow the deceased to partake of the offerings presented to the deities in the major cult temples in the name of the king, particularly on festival occasions. This reversion of offerings displays the importance of official life, particularly in terms of the person of the king, in the relationship between the living and the dead.

The second, personal, function relates more to the private family-based aspects of the funerary cult of the deceased. The private offerings to the dead could be either physical (the offering of food, drink and goods) or verbal (through the utterance of the offering formula); furthermore, these offerings could be perpetuated in pictorial and verbal form (through art and writing). In this way, the offerings made at the burial could be perpetuated by family members (particularly the son and heir), or by people visiting the tomb or passing by the stela.

First of all, here is an example of the offering formula, which you may wish to refer back to as you read over the discussion below:

The offering formula from BM EA 558:

 *ḥtp-dỉ-nsw ꜣsỉr nb ḏdw nṯr ꜥꜣ nb ꜣbḏw*

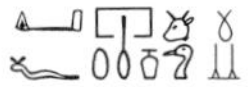 *dỉ=f prt-ḫrw t ḥnḳt kꜣ ꜣpd šs mnḫt*

 *ḫt nb(t) nfr(t) wꜥb(t) ꜥnḫt nṯr ỉm*

 *n kꜣ n ỉmꜣḫ(w) ky*

An offering which the king gives (to) Osiris, lord of Djedu, great god, lord of Abydos, so that he may give a voice offering (in) bread, beer, ox, fowl, alabaster, linen, everything good and pure on which a god lives for the ka of the revered one Key

The most common form of the offering formula is composed of three parts, which can be divided according to the characteristic Egyptian expression found in each:

a.  *ḥtp-dỉ-nsw* an offering which the king gives

b.  *prt-ḫrw* a voice offering

c.  *n kꜣ n* for the ka of

We shall take you through each of these parts in turn, assembling here the material you need to be able to read the standard Osiris offering formula. If you return to this section when reading stelae such as BM EA 587 on p. 46 at the end of this chapter, you should find all the help you need. As you study the various stelae in this book, you will no doubt gain more and more familiarity with the various parts of the offering formula.

a. *The offering to the god(s)*

 *ḥtp-di-nsw* an offering which the king gives

The conventional grouping of this expression uses the following elements:

	from		*nsw*	king
	from	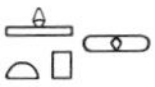	*ḥtp*	offering
	from		*di*	give

(For the writing of the verb 'give', see Exercise 3.5.)

The expression *ḥtp-di-nsw* is often used to refer generally to the offering formula and its associated offering rites (and might less literally be translated as 'the offering rite'). The actual rendering of this stereotypical phrase is notoriously obscure and still exercises the minds of scholars. Whatever its original form, it is clear that by the Middle Kingdom the phrase had come to be treated as a fixed, compound expression. Here we have adopted a standard rendering which we encourage you to follow, rather than trying to work out its meaning from the individual signs.

The name, title and epithets of the god(s)

The name of the god then follows. Note that a word meaning 'to' is not usually written before the god's name, but the sense clearly is that the offerings are made 'to' the god. The god most commonly named in the offering formula (as in the example above) is Osiris and we shall concentrate on him in this chapter. For the other common divine recipient of the offering formula, Anubis, see BM EA 1783 in Chapter 5, and for an example with a number of gods, see BM EA 584 in Chapter 8. The standard names and titles of Osiris are introduced separately in the notes on funerary deities at the end of this chapter.

b. *The offerings are passed on to the deceased*

The voice offering

This section of the offering formula centres around the following expression:

 *prt-ḫrw* a voice offering

The standard writing of *prt-ḫrw* contains the following elements:

	from		*prt*	going out
	from		*ḫrw*	voice
	from	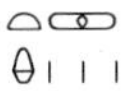	*t*	bread
	from		*ḥnḳt*	beer

The term *prt-ḫrw* is regularly written with the bread and beer signs, even when the voice offering itself is intended without any reference to the bread and beer. They are depicted whether bread and beer are mentioned separately in the subsequent inventory of offerings or not (in which case they may have been thought of as being included within the writing of *prt-ḫrw*).

By the Middle Kingdom *prt-ḫrw* had become a fixed expression used as a cover term for the offerings themselves (and might be loosely translated as 'the ritual offerings'). As a fixed expression, *prt-ḫrw* can even be written with a determinative for the whole phrase, such as 'loaf for offering':

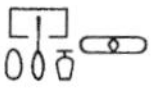 *prt-ḫrw* a voice offering

The second part of the offering formula either starts off with *prt-ḫrw* immediately or marks the passing over of the offerings from the god by the use of:

 *dỉ=f prt-ḫrw* so that he may give a voice offering

dỉ=f is again a form of the verb *rdỉ* 'to give' (see Exercise 3.5). Once again, at this stage we advise you to follow our suggested translation (see Chapter 8 for an explanation).

prt-ḫrw alone is typical of 11th-dynasty stelae. *dỉ=f prt-ḫrw* is more typical from the mid-12th dynasty onwards (*prt-ḫrw* alone being rare by then). During the early part of the 12th dynasty a mixture of both usages is found.

The inventory of offerings:

The offerings are usually enumerated via a standard list of items, usually written with abbreviated writings (given here alongside fuller writings):

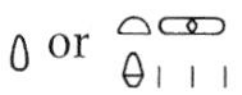	*t*	bread	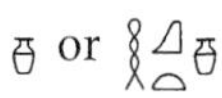	*ḥnḳt*	beer
	*kȝ*	ox		*ȝpd*	fowl
	*šs*	alabaster	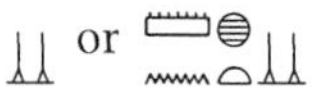	*mnḫt*	linen

Often the offerings are numbered with  *ḫȝ* 'thousand' or  'a thousand of/in'.

The voice offering from the stela of Tjeti:

BM EA 614, Column 1:
prt-ḫrw ḫȝ t ḥnḳt ḫȝ kȝ ȝpd ḫȝ šs mnḫt
A voice offering (of) a thousand bread and beer, a thousand ox and fowl, a thousand alabaster and linen

(*prt-ḫrw* is here written with bread and beer signs but simply read *prt-ḫrw*; contrast with BM EA 558 on p. 36.)

Other offerings sometimes occur (particularly in later 12th- and 13th-dynasty stelae) and are usually more fully written out:

 *mrḥt* oil, unguent

 *sntr* incense

 or 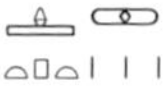 *ḥtp* or *ḥtpt* offerings

 *ḏf(ꜣw)* provisions

The inventory is wrapped up:
As well as listing a standard set of offerings, the offering formula also usually includes a more generic and all-embracing phrase:

 *ḫt nbt nfrt wꜥbt* everything good and pure

You have already studied this expression in Exercise 2.4. It is often qualified by the following fixed expression:

 *ꜥnḫt nṯr im* on which a god lives

Since this is a fixed expression, you should read and translate it as a whole for now, without worrying about its internal grammar (which will be explained in Chapter 7).

c. The recipient of the offering
The deceased recipient of the offering is introduced by one or both of the following phrases:

 *n kꜣ n* for the ka of

 *imꜣḫ(w)* the revered one

In the 11th dynasty and into the early 12th dynasty (after which it dies out), we usually find *imꜣḫ(w)* on its own. The combined usage *n kꜣ n imꜣḫ(w)* begins in the early 12th dynasty and reaches its peak in the mid-12th dynasty. The use of *n kꜣ n* on its own is rare in the early 12th dynasty, but becomes the most common form from the later 12th dynasty onwards.

Once you have reached this point, then you will find the name of the deceased, usually with a title, and ending with the common epithet:

 *mꜣꜥ-ḫrw* the justified

§27 The genitive
The genitive 'of' (as in 'the king of Egypt') occurs in two forms:

a. Direct genitive
The two nouns are put together without any linking word. This construction is only common between closely connected words or in fixed expressions:

	*m-r pr*	overseer of the estate		*nb ꜣbḏw*	lord of Abydos (epithet of Osiris)
	*m-r ꜥḫnwty*	overseer of the chamber		*nb ḏdw*	lord of Djedu (epithet of Osiris)

It also occurs in certain compound expressions, such as those compounded with *ib* 'heart':

 *st-ib* affection, intimacy (literally, situation of the heart)

st-ib occurs in a rather common epithet:

The stela of Ameny identifies his subordinate, Sahathor, with the epithet:

BM EA 162, Central column:

bꜣk=f mꜣꜥ n st-ib=f
His true servant of his affection

b. Indirect genitive

The two nouns are linked by forms of the 'genitival adjective' *n*. This behaves like an adjective and agrees with the preceding noun, taking the following forms:

SINGULAR				PLURAL			
MASCULINE		FEMININE		MASCULINE		FEMININE	
	n		*nt*		*nw*		*nt*

An example occurs in *bꜣk=f mꜣꜥ n st-ib=f* above. Another example occurs in the phrase:

 *n kꜣ n* for the ka of

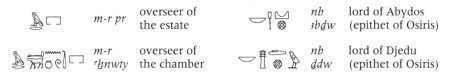

 'of' is written in exactly the same way as the preposition *n* 'to', 'for'. However, in translating into English, one or other of these usually suggests itself (cf. 'for the ka of'). Also there is a tendency for *n* to be used for all numbers and genders, as in *ḥmt=f n st-ib=f* 'his wife of his affection' in Exercise 4.6.

Excursus: Egyptian funerary deities

Osiris

Osiris (*ꜣsir*) was a central figure in the funerary cults of the ancient Egyptians. As noted in Chapter 2, his name is written in an idiosyncratic manner and cannot easily be broken down sign by sign. Indeed there is still some dispute as to the exact reading – in this book we adopt the more recent suggestion to read *ꜣsir* rather than *wsir,* not least since this brings out the parallel with the writing of the name of Isis (for which see p. 42):

 or  *ꜣsir* Osiris — Written with E60-seat above A36-eye for reasons which are still obscure.

The writing of Osiris' name (and the number and nature of his epithets) altered at different periods of Egyptian history, as follows:

 *ꜣsir* — Osiris written without determinative (written with determinative in the 11th dynasty)

 — Alternative writing from the late 12th dynasty

As a 'great god' (*nṯr ꜥꜣ*), the cult of Osiris was celebrated at many shrines, the most important of which are reflected in his titles 'lord of Djedu' and 'lord of Abydos', the writings of which you studied in Exercise 2.2. In BM EA 587 (see Exercise 3.8 below) they are written as follows:

 *nb ḏdw* lord of Djedu (written with graphic transposition, see §21)

 *nṯr ꜥꜣ* great god

 *nb ꜣbḏw* lord of Abydos

These three together represent the classic Middle Kingdom combination of epithets, particularly common in the early 12th dynasty.

The writing of Djedu itself changes over time (as well as sometimes displaying graphic transposition):

 11th – mid-12th dynasty

 or  11th – early 12th dynasty

 late 12th dynasty onward

The pre-eminence of Osiris is reflected in his other name, Khentyimentu (*ḫnty-imntw*), 'the one who is foremost of the westerners' (i.e. the dead gathered in the realm of the setting sun); the name evokes his subjects (the dead spirits) arrayed before his throne:

 *ḫnty-imntw* Khentyimentu

As will become clear from a number of the stelae which you will study in this book, the name Khentyimentu is often included in the offering formula amongst the epithets of Osiris (again typical of the early 12th dynasty).

In mythology, Osiris had been a living king at the beginning of history, but was murdered and dismembered by his ambitious brother, Seth. Osiris' remains were magically restored by Isis (*ꜣst*) – his sister – who was then able to conceive his child, Horus; Horus grew up to defeat Seth and inherit his father's throne in legitimate fashion. Osiris is represented as a deceased king, mummiform but with royal regalia, and a green or black complexion alluding to the fertility of the Nile floodplain.

 or  *ꜣst* Isis  *ḥr* Horus

The passion of Osiris is also reflected in the name Wenennefer (*wnn-nfr*), which means 'the one who continues to be perfect' and hints at his mysterious *post mortem* potency:

 *wnn-nfr* Wenennefer

Wepwawet and Anubis

Funerary stelae from Abydos and elsewhere often invoke Wepwawet and Anubis alongside Osiris. Represented as a dog or jackal, Wepwawet (*wp-wꜣwt*) was an ancient god of Abydos and an active participant in the cult of Osiris: the annual passion-play at Abydos began with the procession of Wepwawet 'to protect his father', Osiris. More generally, Wepwawet was associated with cemeteries and funerals, as reflected in his title 'lord of the sacred land' (*nb tꜣ ḏsr*), where 'sacred land' means the cemetery. Even the name Wepwawet (literally, 'the one who opens the ways', see p. 96) recalls the untrodden paths over the desert along which he guided the souls of the newly deceased to the kingdom of Osiris.

The other major funerary deity was Anubis, whose iconography is close to that of Wepwawet; he also appears in canine form and bears the title 'lord of the sacred land'; his other titles are more obscure. Nevertheless, the funerary gods have distinct roles, apparent in the mythology of the funeral: Anubis embalmed the body of the deceased and conducted the burial ceremonies; Wepwawet led the deceased from this world to the next; and Osiris, king of the dead, represented arrival and rejuvenation in the next life.

Anubis

The name and standard epithets of Anubis:

	*ỉnpw*	Anubis		*tp(y) ḏw=f*	upon his mountain
	*ỉm(y)-wt*	the one in the *wt*		*nb tꜣ ḏsr*	lord of the sacred land

Wepwawet

Wepwawet shares a major epithet with Anubis:

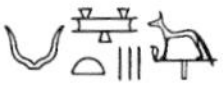	*wp-wꜣwt*	Wepwawet		*nb tꜣ ḏsr*	lord of the sacred land

Exercises

3.1 Signs and words

a. 2-consonant and 3-consonant signs

	*ꜣb* or *mr*		*wn*		*bḥ* or *ḥw*		*ẖn*
	*wꜥ*		*wr*		*nw* or *ỉn*		*ḫnt*

As you will see below, the name of the god Khentyimentu displays the *tw*-bird (B5 long-legged buzzard), a sign which reads *tw* or *tyw* (in this book we shall go for the simpler reading *tw*), but looks similar to the *ꜣ*-bird (B3 Egyptian vulture). The *tw*-bird has a more rounded head, but often the two birds are very similar in writing (sometimes we add a tick to the *tw*-bird to distinguish it). Fortunately the *tw*-bird has a very restricted usage:

 or  *tw*  *ꜣ*

b. Ideograms

	SIGN			EXAMPLE
	E7 feather on standard		*ỉmnt*	the west
	B49 forepart of lion		*ḥꜣt*	front
	E60 seat	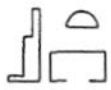	*st*	place, position
	A24 soldier with bow and quiver		*mšꜥ*	army, expedition

Notice that the sign  has appeared in two different words which should not be confused:

 or  *ꜣsỉr* Osiris  *st* place, position

3.2 Words

Transliterate the following words (one uses a sign introduced in an earlier chapter):

 .... great 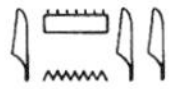 .... Ameny (name)

3.3 Gods' names

You have already been introduced to two forms of Osiris: Khentyimentu and Wenennefer. These are written as follows. Transliterate:

 .... Khentyimentu  .... Wenennefer

3.4 Titles

In the text, the following two titles were introduced. Here they are written in a slightly different way. Transliterate them, using the sign-tables above:

	....	overseer of the chamber		....	sole companion

3.5 Common verbs

Some common verbs are written with otherwise uncommon signs and with some idiosyncracies of their own. It will be useful for you to be familiar with these when reading Chapter 4 (where the presence of (*i*) in brackets will also be explained):

	in(i)	'bring', written with a combination of D33 pot and A57 walking legs, often with sound complement *n*
	ir(i)	'make', 'do', 'act' – written with the 2-consonant sign *ir*
	m33	*m33* 'see', 'look at' – written with determinative placed under *m3*. Some forms of this verb are written with only one *3* – – transliterated *m3*
or	*rdi*	'give', 'place' – A41 arm giving loaf, or E61 conical loaf. Without *r* as or , transliterated *di*. From the hieratic, also written with arm as *rdi* or *di*

3.6 The offering formula from BM EA 162

BM EA 162
(carved limestone; w. 75cm)

The offering formula is usually written in a telegram-like style with very abbreviated writings and certain prepositions omitted. The top portion of the stela of Ameny (BM EA 162), however, rather unusually provides us with a more fully written out version of certain sections of the offering formula.

Transliterate and translate, using the template provided in the text (§26 above), and study the individual writings of the various component parts of the formula. You should also make use of the vocabulary introduced in the other exercises above.

VOCABULARY

	*ỉr-n*	born of		*=f*	he, his (pronoun)
	*m-r mšʿ wr*	general-in-chief		*ḫr*	before, in front of
	*ḳbw*	Qebu (name)			

Notes:

i *ỉr-n* means 'whom such-and-such a person made' but this is not a satisfactory idiom in English.

ii *m-r mšʿ wr* means literally 'great overseer of the army'.

iii In line 1, the damaged hieroglyphs are part of the standard epithets of Osiris: *ḫnty-ỉmntw* (with an extra *tw*-bird), *nṯr ʿ3, nb 3bḏw* (see p. 41).

3.7 Offering table scene

Meir I, pl. 9

In scenes, the offerings are often shown placed on a table before the deceased. Transliterate and translate the hieroglyphs below the offering table scene from the tomb of Senbi (consult the section on the offering formula if necessary).

VOCABULARY

	ḥ3ty-ʿ	governor, mayor		*ḫ3(w)*	thousands

The laden offering table constituting the 'funerary meal' for the deceased is referred to as:

or *dbḥt-ḥtp* the required offerings

3.8 Study exercise: BM EA 587

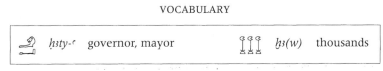

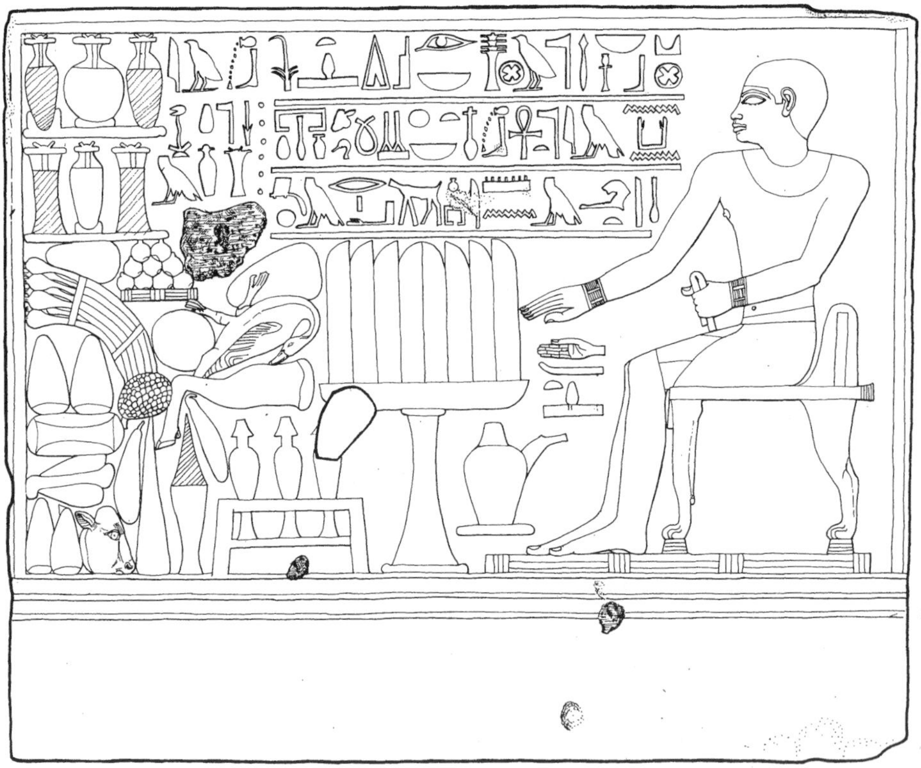

BM EA 587
(carved and painted limestone; H. 56cm)

It is now time for you to study your first stela – BM EA 587, the funerary monument of the overseer of the chamber Amenemhet. Transliterate and translate the hieroglyphs written within the registers (and not those accompanying the vases at the top left, written without registers). You should consult the sections on the offering formula in the text (§26) where necessary. You may also find it useful to read through the notes on Osiris given on pp. 40–42.

VOCABULARY

	*m-r* *ꜥḫnw(ty)*	overseer of the chamber		*ỉmn-m-ḥꜣt*	Amenemhet

(See p. 102 for some remarks on the title *m-r ꜥḫnwty*.)

Notice that the inscription has been carefully laid out: the *ḥtp-dỉ-nsw* formula takes up the first line; the *prt-ḫrw* formula the second line and the epithets, name and titles of the stela owner the third line.

3.9 Study exercise: BM EA 585

BM EA 585, shown on the next page, has another standard offering formula, this time written from right to left.

a. Translation

Transliterate and translate, using the notes and vocabulary below.

Notice how the names of Sarenenutet and his mother Bameket are written to fit the space available. The scenes and figures are in raised relief and the inscriptions in sunk relief. The element *-mkt* in the mother's name is written in the scene area and in raised relief.

VOCABULARY

	*bꜣ-mkt*	Bameket		*ms-n*	born of
	*nṯrw*	gods		*ḥsb šnwty*	counter of the double granaries
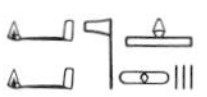	*dd ḥtp-nṯr*	offering-giver		*sꜣ-rnnwtt*	Sarenenutet

b. Epigraphy

Compare this stela with BM EA 587:

i Identify the differences in the shape and arrangement of particular hieroglyphs (you may also wish to consider the figures and the offering tables).

ii Identify the differences in the phraseology of the offering formula.

BM EA 585
(carved limestone; H. 52cm)

Chapter 4

Scenes and captions

The first part of this book was dedicated primarily to building up your knowledge of the hieroglyphic signs needed to equip you for the twin goals of reading the names of the kings and the offering formula. In this part of the book we will move on to broaden your knowledge of the ancient Egyptian language and how it works, equipping you to read a wider range of Middle Kingdom stelae in the British Museum and elsewhere, and also supplying you with a firm foundation for moving on to study the wealth of surviving ancient Egyptian writings.

§28 Captions: the infinitive

Verbs typically label actions or events such as 'do', or 'kick', though some verbs label states or conditions such as 'remain'. A major topic to be dealt with in reading hieroglyphs is how to get the right translation of verbs according to whether they refer to actions in the past, present or future. Over the next few chapters we will equip you to bring this degree of accuracy to your translations.

A good place to start is with scenes and captions. Scenes are often accompanied by captions which very conveniently label the action:

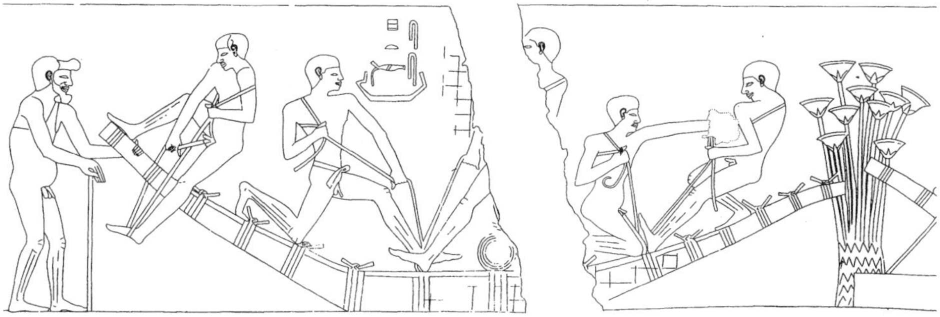

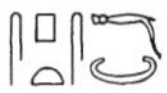 *spt smḥ* Binding a skiff (Meir II, pl. 4)

(In captions, words are often written without determinatives, since the image itself pictures the meaning.)

In English the *-ing* form of the verb translates rather well here, whereas using the simple English past 'bound a skiff' seems a little incomplete and unsatisfactory. Exactly the same is true in Egyptian. In such captions, Egyptian uses a particular form of the verb which, as you will see in the next chapter, differs markedly from the form for expressing the past. In Egyptian the equivalent of the *-ing* form in this usage is termed the *infinitive* (see §31 below for its forms).

Before we progress further, there is one general comment we would like to make. The terms for the various Egyptian verb-forms are now rather traditional; they are not always very clear in their meaning, nor do they always agree with the use of the same term in describing the grammar of English. So the term 'infinitive' and its meaning is not really important – it will, however, serve as a convenient label by which we can readily refer to the verb-form.

When the actor is mentioned in an Egyptian caption, this is usually introduced by *ỉn* 'by':

Before the figure of the owner is a lengthy adoration caption, the bare bones of which are:

BM EA 567: *sn tꜣ n ḫnty-ỉmntw m prt ꜥꜣt ... ỉn ỉmꜣḫ(w) m-r šnꜥw ỉmn-m-ḥꜣt*
Kissing the ground to Khentyimentu in the great procession ... by the revered one, the overseer of the provisioning area Amenemhet

For the vocabulary, see the next section and the excursus on titles, p. 103.

§29 Adoration

The owner of a stela often expressed a wish to participate in certain important festivals beyond death, particularly the Osiris Mysteries (for which see pp. 54–56). He either wished to participate in them directly – through seeing (*mꜣꜣ*), adoring (*dwꜣ*), kissing the ground (*sn tꜣ*), or giving praise (*dỉt ỉꜣw*) to the god – or through having offerings made to him at such times. For example:

The vertical columns of stela BM EA 580 comprise a hymn to Osiris which begins:

BM EA 580, Lines 1-2: *dỉt ỉꜣw n ꜣsỉr sn tꜣ n wp-wꜣwt*
Giving praise to Osiris, kissing the ground to Wepwawet

§30 Verb classes and the infinitive

So how does this all work? The first and most basic point is that when deciding on the exact translation to be adopted (for example, should we translate 'kissing' in the example above as opposed to 'kissed' or 'will kiss'?), two points should be borne in mind:

i what help does the writing of the verb give us? (the question of *form*)

ii how does the verb fit in the context of the inscription? (the question of *function*)

As you will see, since hieroglyphs only write consonants and not vowels, the hieroglyphic writing alone will not always direct us to the exact form. However, once we take into account how the verb seems to be being used in the inscription, then we can usually get good sense out of it. The first 'tool of the trade' that we need to introduce you to is the topic of verb classes. All the verbs in ancient Egyptian can be gathered into a small number of groups, which, when considered as a whole (or *paradigm*), usually allow us to see each form somewhat more clearly. The following are the standard verb classes with a convenient example for each class:

VERB CLASS		EXAMPLE AND DESCRIPTION			
STRONG VERBS	e.g.		*sḏm*	to hear	stem does not usually show any alteration
DOUBLING VERBS	e.g.		*mꜣꜣ*	to see	stem ends in a double consonant
WEAK VERBS	e.g.		*mr(i͗)*	to love	stem ends with a 'weak' consonant, usually *-i͗*
EXTRA WEAK VERBS	e.g.		*rdi͗*	to give	chiefly verbs with two or three weak consonants

Notes

i With weak verbs, the final *-i͗* is usually omitted in writing and therefore in transliteration. For practical reasons, however, we will transliterate the extra weak verb 'to give' as *rdi͗* or *di͗*.

ii Extra weak verbs behave like ordinary weak verbs, but sometimes show additional features.

The stem of a strong verb is not usually that helpful since it rarely shows any differences. As you will see below, the infinitive of strong verbs gives us little written clue. Doubling verbs have a root which ends with the same consonant repeated twice. In writing, some forms of these verbs show only one of these consonants (e.g. *mꜣ*) and in other forms show two (e.g. *mꜣꜣ*) and this can help in distinguishing certain forms. Weak and extra weak verbs, whose roots end in a 'weak consonant' (*-i͗* or *-w*), are the most interesting because they show a wider range of variation in different verb-forms, which can be most useful in spotting a particular form (we shall see that weak verb infinitives are rather more easy to spot than strong verb infinitives).

One important point to note about weak verbs is that the *-i* and *-w* with which their root or dictionary forms end do not usually appear in writing and so need not be transliterated. However, so that you can see readily whether a verb is a weak verb or not, the *-i* or *-w* of weak verbs will be added in brackets (as in the table above) in the vocabularies in this book.

§31 The forms of the infinitive

So let's turn to the infinitive and see how all this works out. The infinitive in Egyptian has the following form:

	INFINITIVE		
STRONG VERBS - no change		*sḏm*	hearing
DOUBLING VERBS - doubling		*mꜣꜣ*	seeing
WEAK VERBS - end in *-t*		*mrt*	loving
EXTRA WEAK VERBS - end in *-t*	 or 	*rdit* or *dit*	giving/placing (*r* optional in both writings, see p. 44)

Here are some examples to illustrate this:

STRONG VERBS	Meir I, pl. 2:	 *ꜥmꜥꜣ r ꜣpd(w)* Throwing at the birds
DOUBLING VERBS	Meir I, pl. 9:	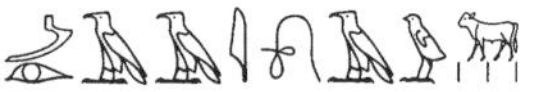 *mꜣꜣ iwꜣw* Seeing the cattle
WEAK VERBS	Meir II, pl. 4:	 *spt smḥ* Binding a skiff
EXTRA WEAK VERBS	BM EA 580, 1:	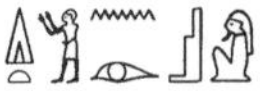 *dit iꜣw n ꜣsir* Giving praise to Osiris

The most noticeable feature of the table is that the form of the infinitive of weak verbs ends in a *-t*. Consider again the scene and caption with which we introduced this chapter (repeated on p. 53).

If you look at the vocabulary at the end of the book, you will find the following word listed:

 *sp(i)* bind (together)

(D11 coil of rope is a common determinative for ropes, cords and actions performed with them.)

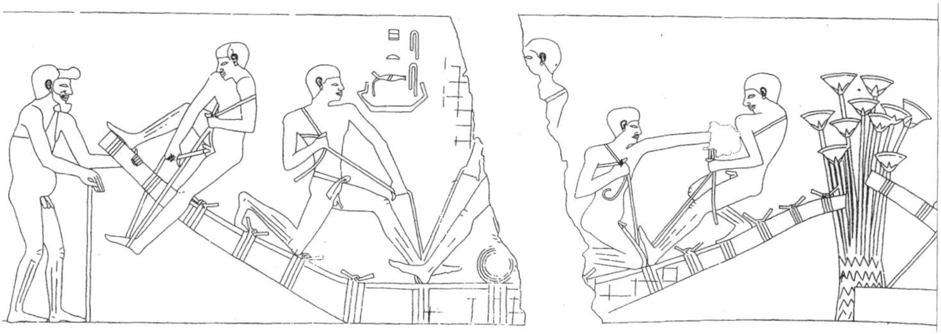

spt smḥ Binding a skiff

Just like English dictionaries, dictionaries and word-lists of ancient Egyptian just give you a standard citation form (the *root*), here *sp(ỉ)* 'bind (together)', and do not tell whether you need 'binding', 'bound' or whatever in your actual translation. All the citation form tells us is that *sp(ỉ)* is a **weak verb**. But if we look at the actual example we find the following form, showing an extra *-t*:

spt binding

and also, of course, it is being used in a caption. Together this information allows us to decide that *spt* is an example of the Egyptian infinitive and can be translated well into English as 'bind-**ing**'.

We advise you at this stage to follow our example here in adhering to a small number of suggested *translation schemes* for the various forms we will introduce you to, since this will help you to get good sense out of the hieroglyphic inscriptions you will read in this book. At first, it is better to refrain from trying to be more imaginative or to 'guestimate' the meaning. So our first translation scheme is for the infinitive (simply substitute the necessary verb for 'do'):

infinitive translation scheme **doing** or **to do**

In the examples in this chapter 'doing' will be the right choice, but on other occasions 'to do' will fit better. If the range of meaning seems a bit loose, compare the English '**To study** hieroglyphs is interesting' with '**Studying** hieroglyphs is interesting' where the English 'to do' and 'doing' forms have a similar usage.

Now, of course, infinitives of strong and doubling verbs do not offer us much help in their writing. But the context and sometimes other parallel examples can help out. As an example, we can consider again the fishing and fowling scene from the tomb of Senbi which you studied in edited form in Chapter 1 and which you can study in its original, complete form as Exercise 4.6. The two edited labels were:

a. Scene of spearing fish:

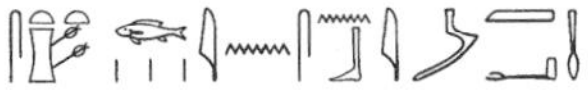

Meir I, pl. 2: *stt rm(w) ỉn snbỉ mꜣꜥ-ḫrw*
Spearing fish by Senbi, the justified

b. Scene of throwing the throw-stick at the birds:

Meir I, pl. 2: *ꜥmꜥꜣ r ꜣpd(w) ỉn snbỉ mꜣꜥ-ḫrw*
Throwing at the birds by Senbi, the justified

st(ỉ) 'spear' is a weak verb, hence the infinitive *stt* 'spearing'. *ꜥmꜥꜣ*, however, is a strong verb and does not provide a particularly helpful writing. Yet the context of the caption and the parallel with the other caption showing us *stt* 'spearing' urge us to consider the infinitive and the translation 'throw**ing**'. Notice also how using the suggested translation scheme helps us to draw together a decent English translation of the whole: 'throwing at the birds by Senbi the justified', whereas reasonable alternatives such as 'throws at the birds' do not: 'throws at the birds by Senbi the justified' is not particularly good English.

Excursus: The cult of Osiris at Abydos

The heart of the cult of Osiris at Abydos was the annual festival at which his cult-statue was brought, in a ritual boat carried aloft by priests, in procession from his temple to his supposed tomb at Umm el-Qaꜥab ('mother of pots'). The festival procession had two fundamental components – a public section during which the divine image passed through the cemetery abutting the temple's western side, and a private section out in the desert where the secret rites concerning the mysteries and passion of Osiris were performed. During the Middle Kingdom at Abydos, members of the élite dedicated stelae, or erected offering chapels as cenotaphs, hoping to ensure their continued participation in the festival after their own death. The cemetery at Abydos was therefore a veritable city of the dead with a wealth of monuments, and, as you will see, Abydene stelae form an important body of the Middle Kingdom monuments studied in this book.

Here we shall concentrate on the route of the festival. In Exercise 6.5, you will study one of the principal surviving ancient sources for the festival procession itself. The exact location and scope of the various Egyptian place names used are still a matter for debate. However, the map below gives a plausible version.

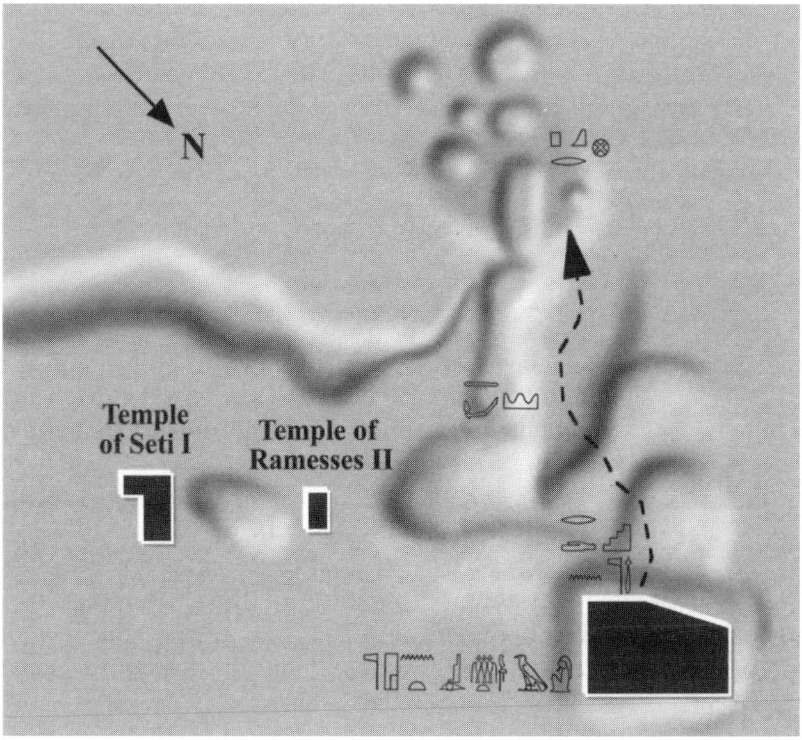

The starting point of the festival procession was the Osiris Temple ( ), housing the statue of the god. As you will see for yourself in Exercise 6.5, there were actually two outward processions – the 'procession of Wepwawet' ( ) and then the 'great procession' of Osiris ( ). Stelae were concentrated near the western entrance to the temple, in an area of high ground known as the 'terrace of the great god' ( ), so that the deceased could look upon the emergence and return of the gods (hence the references to 'kissing the ground' and 'giving praise' as the images of the gods pass by – the cult images of the gods are often referred to as their *nfrw* 'splendour'). The procession crossed the terrace before descending into a wadi (the sacred land,). The god then proceeded out into the desert on the God's boat-journey ( ) to Poker ( ) where the divine mysteries and rites were performed. Abydos had a long history as one of the most sacred sites in the country since it was at Umm el-Qaʿab that the earliest kings were buried. By the 12th

Dynasty, the tomb of the 1st-dynasty king Djer was believed to be that of Osiris himself.

VOCABULARY

	*prt*	procession	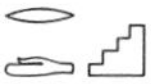	*rwd*	terrace
	*prt ꜥꜣt*	the great procession		*ḥwt-nṯr*	temple
	*prt wp-wꜣwt*	the procession of Wepwawet		*tꜣ ḏsr*	sacred land
	*pḳr*	Poker		*ḏꜣt nṯr*	god's boat-journey

Exercises

4.1 Signs

a. Sound signs:

	*in*		*sn*		*wḥm*
	*ḥm*		*m(w)t*		*dwꜣ*

b. Determinatives:

SIGN		EXAMPLE		
	F6 basin combined with canopy	 or 	*ḥb*	festival
	A20 man with arms in adoration	 or 	*iꜣ(w)*	praise, adoration

Both of these determinatives are used widely, for various festivals and for words to do with praise and supplication. Note, however, that when used on their own, they are abbreviated writings of the two specific words given.

4.2 Words

Transliterate the following words:

	....	sister		....	wife
	....	adore, praise		....	kiss
	....	brother		....	repeat

4.3 Translation

Transliterate and translate the two captions on the following page:

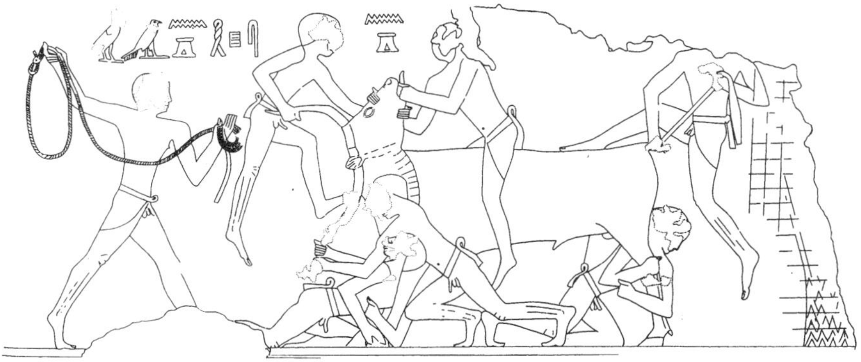

Meir II, pl. 4

The bull is also labelled separately between the two figures at the top.

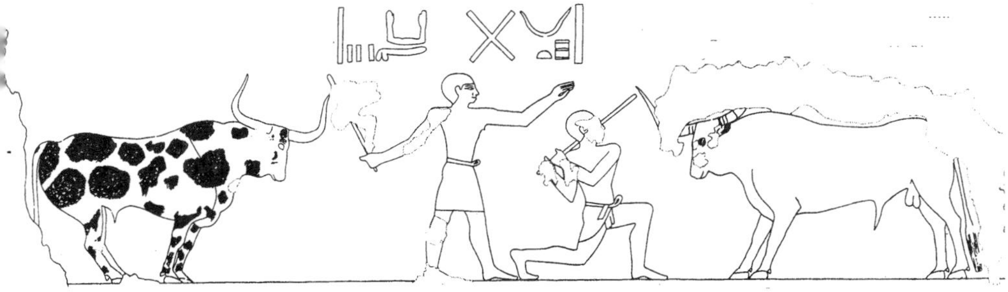

Meir I, pl. 11

VOCABULARY (NORMALISED WRITINGS)

	wp(ỉ)	separate, open	or	*ngꜣw*	long-horned bull
	spḥ	lassoo		*kꜣ*	bull

4.4 Translation

Transliterate and translate the following sections from the top of BM EA 101, the stela of Nebipusenwosret, dating from the reign of Amenemhet III (shown on the next page – ignore the sections in grey). You may wish to read the notes on the cult of Osiris at Abydos on pp. 54–56 for useful background information.

The following notes will help you in translating the central section:

Notes

i The eye emblem in the centre can be read as a verb 'to see'. It is thought to read *ptr* 'to see, view', rather than *mꜣꜣ*. The form is the infinitive.

ii See §§17–18 on the king's name and epithets (the epithets are divided into two columns mirroring the general division into a section on Osiris on the left and one on Wepwawet on the right). *mry* is used in the epithet 'beloved of the god X'. The name of the god (and his titles) are written first for reasons of prestige (as noted in §22 above).

BM EA 101
(carved and painted limestone; W. 66cm)

The deceased king Senwosret III forms the central focus of the scene. As recorded in the middle section of the stela, Nebipusenwosret had this stela sent to Abydos in the care of the elder lector-priest Ibi who had come, as part of the priesthood of the temple of Abydos, to the residence of the then reigning king Amenemhet III.

VOCABULARY

	prt	procession		*ptr nfrw*	viewing the splendour
	=f	his		*m*	in, during
	nb(=i)-pw-snwsrt	Nebipu-senwosret		*nfr*	perfect, wonderful
	nfrw	perfection, beauty, wonder, splendour		*ḥb(w)*	festivals
	dwꜣ	adore, praise		*ḏt r nḥḥ*	enduringly and repeatedly

Grammar

As noted in §10, adjectives follow and agree with their nouns. Exercise 4.4 provides examples of feminine and plural agreement (cf. §§8 and 15 above):

	*prt=f nfrt*	his wonderful procession
	*prt ꜥ3t*	the great procession
	*ḥb(w)=f nfrw*	his wonderful festivals

4.5 Translation

Transliterate and translate the following sections from BM EA 581, one of the three stelae of the overseer of the chamber Intef son of Senet in the British Museum. These stelae are extremely elaborate in their wording, so we will only consider two sections. Ignore the parts in grey.

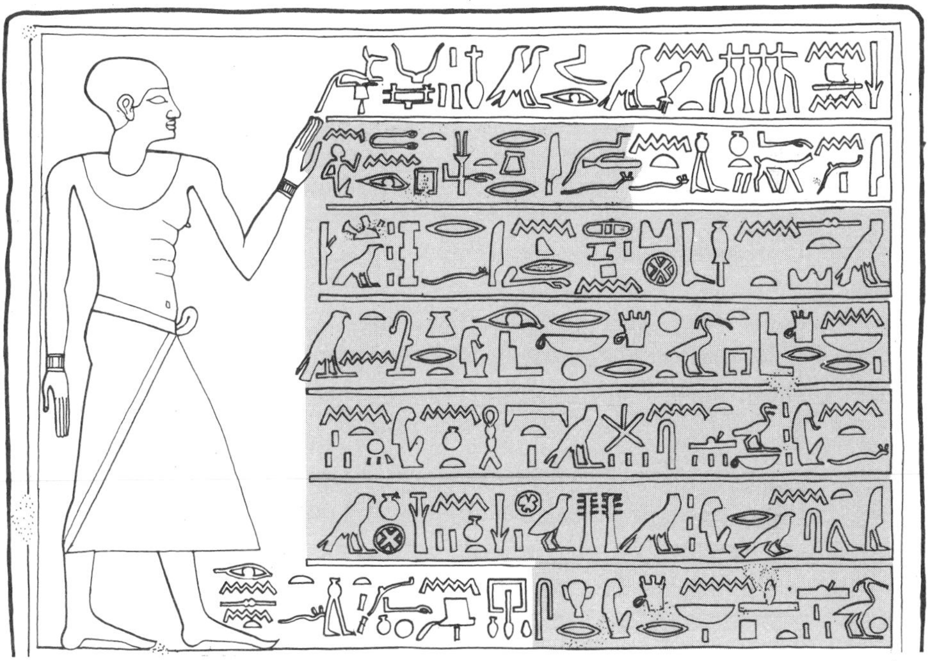

BM EA 581
(carved limestone; W. 36cm)

VOCABULARY

	*intf*	Intef		*ir-n*	born of
	*m33*	see, look at		*nfrw*	splendour, wonder
	*sn*	kiss		*snt*	Senet
	t3	land, ground			

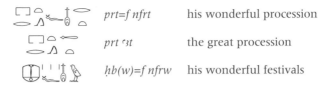

Writings

The extracts from BM EA 581 show two variant writings worth noting:

 and 	*ḫnty-imntw*	Khentyimentu	The first sign has two variants, with three or four pots (E38, E39)
 and 	*m-r ꜥḫnwty*	overseer of the chamber	*ḫ* and *ẖ* are similar sounds and can occur in variant writings

4.6 Study exercise: Fishing and fowling scene from the tomb of Senbi at Meir

You are now in a position to transliterate and translate the original version of the fishing and fowling scene from the tomb of Senbi shown on page 61.

VOCABULARY

	*ꜣpd(w)*	fowl, birds		*nb* and *nbt*	lord, possessor (m.), lady, possessor (f.)
	*ib*	heart		*r*	at, towards
	*imꜣḫ*	reverence		*rm(w)*	fish
	*imꜣḫy*	revered one		*ḥꜣty-ꜥ*	governor
	*imntt*	western		*ḥmt*	wife
	*in*	by		*ḫr*	before
	*ꜣsir*	Osiris		*ḫtmty-bity*	seal-bearer of the king
	*ꜥmꜥꜣ*	throw		*smyt*	desert
	*=f*	his		*smr wꜥt(y)*	sole companion
 or 	*mꜣꜥ-ḫrw*	justified		*snbi*	Senbi
	*m-r ḥm-nṯr*	overseer of priests		*st-ib*	affection, intimacy
	*mrs*	Meres		*st(i)*	spear

Notes

i Fishing scene: ancient correction at end of line, read: .

ii Fowling scene: end of first line, read . Above wife, read *n* 'of' above .

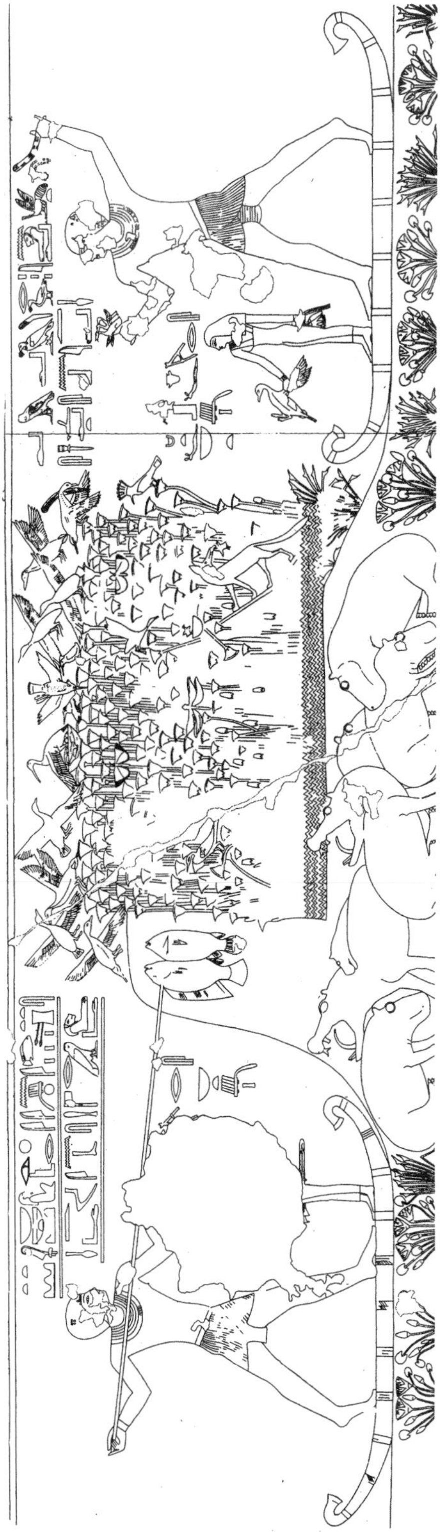

(Meir I, pl. 2)

4.7 Study exercise: The coffin of Nakhtankh (BM EA 35285)

Although in this book we concentrate on stelae in the British Museum, the material that you are working through also puts you in a position to study inscriptions on other kinds of museum objects, particularly where they include the offering formula. In this exercise you will study the inscriptions on the outside of a Middle Kingdom coffin (BM EA 35285, the coffin of Nakhtankh).

We shall concentrate on the two exterior sides of the coffin, omitting the inscriptions on the head and foot ends. The inscriptions are aligned on the coffin as follows:

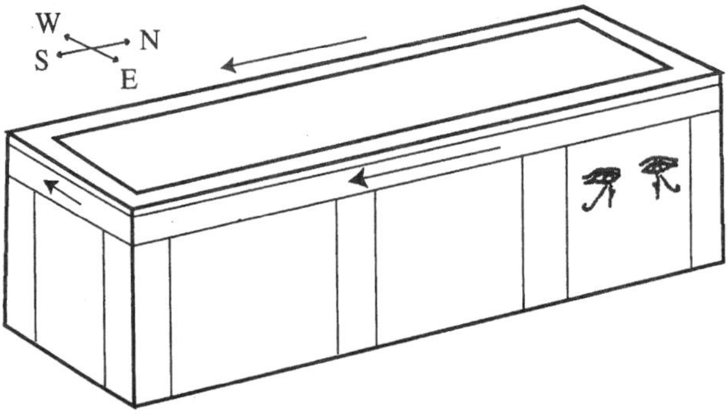

The body was laid on its left side, facing towards the east, in order to be able to look out through the eyes on the eastern side towards the newly rejuvenated sun at sunrise. Hence the inscriptions run from the head at the northern end towards the feet at the southern end. This represents the typical arrangement of a Middle Kingdom rectangular coffin. On the eastern side (the side with the eyes looking out towards the sunrise), the main inscription is an offering formula to Osiris. On the western side is an offering formula to Anubis. At the corners, the inscriptions invoke the four sons of Horus, protective deities for the body of the deceased (with the classic Middle Kingdom arrangement of Imseti and Duamutef on the east side and Hapy and Qebehsenuef on the west). The central columns invoke deities closely linked to Osiris: Shu and Geb on the east side and their female consorts Tefnet and Nut on the west.

The eastern side

The eastern side of the coffin is shown on the next page. Transliterate and translate with the help of the vocabulary and notes below:

BM EA 35285 (eastern side)
(painted wood; L. 212cm)

Notes

i *ỉmꜣḫ(y) ḫr* displays haplography (i.e., where the last sign in one word and the first in the next are the same and the sign is written only once).

ii *mꜣꜥ-ḫrw* is (a) written occasionally with the papyrus-roll and (b) omitted in the northernmost column.

iii the *gb*-goose (B8) is different from the *sꜣ*-duck (B7).

VOCABULARY

nḫt-ꜥnḫ	Nakhtankh
ḫnt(y)-ỉmntw	Khentyimentu

THE FOUR SONS OF HORUS

ỉmstỉ	Imseti
dwꜣ-mwt=f	Duamutef
ḥpy	Hapy
ḳbḥ-snw=f	Qebehsenuef

OTHER DEITIES

šw	Shu
gb	Geb
tfnt	Tefnet
nwt	Nut

The western side

The principal inscription on the western side of the coffin is an offering formula to Anubis. Whereas the Osiris offering formula concerns the offerings to sustain the ka of the deceased, the Anubis offering formula concerns the burial itself.

Transliterate and translate with the help of the following notes:

BM EA 35285 (western side)

Notes

i The standard organization of the Anubis offering formula is: *ḥtp-dỉ-nsw* followed by Anubis with his epithets and then *ḳrst nfrt* without being introduced by *dỉ=f*. You may wish to introduce your translation of *ḳrst nfrt* with a dash or colon after the *ḥtp-dỉ-nsw* section.

ii Read *ỉs=f nfr n ẖrt-nṯr* with the indirect genitive (see §27 above). *ỉs=f* means 'his tomb'; for *=f* see §33.

iii Anubis is invoked with his standard epithets (see p. 42) and a further epithet:

ḫnty sḥ-nṯr the one before the divine booth

VOCABULARY

ỉs	tomb	*nfr*	good, perfect, wonderful
ẖrt-nṯr	cemetery, necropolis	*ḳrst*	burial

Chapter 5

Description

In the next two chapters, we will introduce you to the past tense, concentrating on inscriptions in which the deceased reflects back upon, and describes, his official life. We will also introduce you to the ancient Egyptian pronouns.

§32 Introduction: description

In a typical type of funerary inscription – which we can term *self-presentation* – the owner presents himself (rarely, herself) according to the ethical values of Middle Kingdom élite society and in terms of success and achievement, particularly in royal service. In order to *describe* the *activities* which the official participated in, the *tasks* he accomplished, and his *ethical behaviour*, the past tense is generally used.

The official Intef son of Senet proclaims his ethical behaviour:

BM EA 562, Line 10:

iw ḳrs.n=i ỉꜣ(w)
I buried the old

This construction comprises the past form of the verb ( *ḳrs* + *.n*; cf. English 'bury' + '-ed' – see §33 below) *followed* by the subject ('I') and other elements; the sentence begins with an auxiliary  *iw* which is not translated into English (see §34 below).

§33 The past: *sḏm.n(=f)*

The past form is termed the  *sḏm.n(=f)* (pronounced 'sedjemenef') 'he heard', using the verb *sḏm* 'to hear' in the 'he' form ('he heard') as the standard example. In this form, an affix *.n* '-ed', is added to the verb-stem (written after the determinative). As a standard convention, in transliteration the *.n* is usually separated from the stem of the verb by a dot – this just makes it easier to spot. The forms of the *sḏm.n(=f)* for the verb classes (§30 above) are:

sḏm.n(=f)

STRONG VERBS		*sḏm.n=f*	he heard
DOUBLING VERBS		*mꜣ.n=f* no doubling	he saw
WEAK VERBS		*mr.n=f*	he loved
EXTRA WEAK VERBS		*(r)dỉ.n=f* *r* optional	he gave

When there is a pronoun subject (e.g. 'I heard', 'he heard'), the *suffix pronouns* are used (see §36 below); the pronouns for 'I' and 'he' are given here (compare with the example above):

SUFFIX PRONOUNS   *sḏm.n(=f)*

I		=ỉ		*sḏm.n=ỉ*	I heard
He/It		=f		*sḏm.n=f*	he heard

The suffix pronouns (see the reference tables on p. 148 for a full list) attach to the verb; this is indicated in transliteration by the symbol '='. Once again this has the practical value of making the suffix pronouns easy to spot in transliteration: *sḏm.n=f* is much easier to read (*sḏm* 'hear' + *.n* '-d' + *=f* 'he') than *sḏmnf*.

With an ordinary noun subject (e.g. 'the man heard'), the noun follows the verb, but does not fix onto it (hence there is no '=' in transliteration):

Hekaib records an inspection of his property by the ruler:

BM EA 167,
Line 10:   *ỉw ỉp.n ḥkꜣ ỉwꜣ(w)(=ỉ)*
              The ruler inspected my cattle

(For the omission of *=ỉ* in *ỉwꜣ(w)=ỉ* 'my cattle', see §35 below; see p. 73 for vocabulary.)

§34 Auxiliaries

The *sḏm.n(=f)* is usually preceded by an auxiliary such as 〔〕 *ỉw*. In stela inscriptions *ỉw sḏm.n(=f)* often translates well as a simple past ('someone did something'):

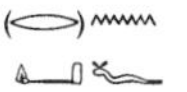

Inhuretnakht extols his proper conduct as a responsible official:

BM EA 1783, Line 4:

ỉw rdỉ.n(=ỉ) t n ḥḳr ḥbs(w) n ḥꜣy
I gave bread to the hungry and clothes to the naked

(There is no word for 'and' in Egyptian; for vocabulary, see Exercise 5.4.)

There is no simple English equivalent for *ỉw* and so it is left untranslated. It invokes a sense of involvement in the assessment or presentation of what is said/written. In self-presentation inscriptions, *ỉw sḏm.n(=f)* gives a sense of looking back over one's life. In other contexts the perfect ('someone has done something') also suits, particularly in recorded speech.

§35 Omission of the first person suffix pronoun

The first person suffix pronoun ('I-me-my') is sometimes omitted in writing, particularly in texts where a figure of the person is present (e.g. stelae and tomb inscriptions) or strongly implied (e.g. where the text is all about that person):

Another of Inhuretnakht's stated ethical acts:

BM EA 1783, Lines 4-5:

ỉw ḏꜣ.n(=ỉ) ỉww <m> mẖnt(=ỉ) ḏs(=ỉ)
I ferried the boatless in my own ferry

Note:

i *ỉww* 'the boatless' is written with a doubling of the 2-consonant sign  B32.

ii Repeated consonants are sometimes omitted: here only one *m* is written in *m mẖnt(=ỉ)* 'in my ferry'.

iii *ḏs* is used for the emphatic reflexive '(my/him)self' or 'own'.

§36 Suffix pronouns

Although, as we shall see, there are different sets of pronouns in Egyptian (see §41 and §49), they are not always used in the same way as the different sets of pronouns in English. For example, the suffix pronoun *=ỉ* may be translated into English by any of 'I' or 'me' or 'my' as appropriate. The suffix pronouns are used:

a. As the subjects of verbs ('I', 'he')

The official Intef son of Senet proclaims his ethical behaviour:

BM EA 562, Line 10:

ỉw ḳrs.n=ỉ ỉꜣ(w)
I buried the old

b. As the possessor of a noun ('my', 'his')

The top part of BM EA 101 behind the figure of Nebipusenwosret (see p. 58):

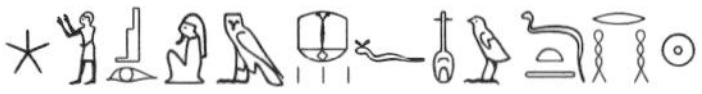

BM EA 101: *dwꜣ ꜣsỉr m ḥb(w)**=f** nfrw ḏt r nḥḥ*
Adoring Osiris in **his** wonderful festivals enduringly and repeatedly

c. As the object after a preposition ('me', 'him')

From the Abydos formula on BM EA 162:

BM EA 162, Line 5: *ḏd.t(w) n**=f** ỉw m ḥtp ỉn wr(w) n ꜣbḏw*
May 'Welcome in peace' be said for **him** by the great of Abydos

(For the meaning of *ḏd.t(w)*, see p. 115.)

For the full list of suffix pronouns, see Reference table, p. 148.

§37 The past relative form: *sḏmt.n(=f)*

The following paragraph discusses a more advanced point which some of you may wish to work through at this stage in order to gain the maximum understanding of the inscriptions read as study exercises to this chapter. Others may consider these points a little abstruse at this stage and may prefer to return to this paragraph later on.

As well as being *described* ('someone did something'), events can also be *characterised* (treated as a 'thing which someone did': 'what/which someone did'). Egyptian has a special way of characterising an event – by using the *relative forms* – which is quite different from English and is often seen as one of the more difficult aspects of ancient Egyptian. However, the use of the relative forms is extremely common and will crop up in a number of examples, and so we will attempt to open up this area of Egyptian for you by the use of our notion of a translation scheme. The difference between description and characterisation can be seen in the following example:

The self-presentation of Inhuretnakht ends:

BM EA 1783, Line 5: *ỉw ỉr.n(=ỉ) kꜣw 100 m ỉrt.n(=ỉ) ḏs(=ỉ)*
I acquired 100 bulls through what I did myself

Notes

- i 𓍢 is the number 100.
- ii *m* here has the meaning 'through' or 'by the means of'.
- iii *ỉr(ỉ)* 'to do' has a wide range of idiomatic meanings.
- iv *=ỉ* is omitted (see §35 above).

In Egyptian, the described event 'I acquired 100 bulls' is expressed by using the *sḏm.n(=f)* form *ỉr.n(=ỉ)*. However, the characterised event 'what I did myself' is expressed by using another verb-form – *the past relative form: ỉrt.n(=ỉ)*. In this usage, there is no separate word for 'what' or 'which', rather the verb-form shows a *-t* in its writing, so *ỉrt.n(=ỉ)* in itself means 'what I did' without needing extra words. Notice that missing out a word such as 'what' in translation leaves the sentence with poor sense: 'I acquired a hundred bulls through I did myself'. You will often find this to be the case: the relative forms (and their cousins, the participles introduced in Chapter 7) scream out for the inclusion of an English word such as 'what' or 'which' in translation. The same stela provides another similar example:

Between the figures of Inhuretnakht and Hui, the following dedication label about the stela appears:

BM EA 1783: *ỉrt.n -n=f sꜣ=f smsw=f mry=f dbỉ*
What his eldest and beloved son Debi **made** for him

Notes

i *-n=f* precedes *sꜣ=f smsw=f mry=f* in word order.
ii In *sꜣ=f smsw=f mry=f* both *smsw* and *mry* share the following *=f* and the phrase means literally 'his son, his eldest, his beloved'.

In this book we shall focus on the relative form only when it shows the extra *-t*. In this way we can isolate the following convenient translation schemes for the past *sḏm.n(=f)* form and the past relative form *sḏmt.n(=f)* discussed in this chapter:

PAST TENSE		*ỉr.n=f*	he did
PAST RELATIVE FORM	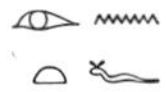	*ỉrt.n=f*	what he did

Excursus: Names and kinship terms

Names and family relationships play an important role on funerary stelae. We present here a number of the names to be found on the monuments studied in this book, and the kinship terms used, for you to refer to. As the section on names indicates, many Egyptian names (like our own) have a meaning. Nevertheless, in translating Egyptian monuments, it is better to stick to the name itself, rather than trying to translate the name into English.

Names

Names referring to personal condition

In a society with high infant mortality, it is not surprising that many names reflect anxiety about new-born children or wishes for their future health:

	Senbi (Meir tomb-chapel B, No. 1)	*snbi*	healthy
	Nakhti (BM EA 143)	*nḫti*	strong, vigorous
	Khu (BM EA 571)	*ḫw*	protected

Names referring to deities

One type associates the individual directly with a deity:

	Isis (BM EA 143)	*ꜣst*

A second type invokes a close – often familial – relationship with a god:

	Sarenenutet (BM EA 585)	*sꜣ-rnnwtt*	son of Renenutet
	Satsobek (BM EA 586)	*sꜣt-sbk*	daughter of Sobek
	Senwosret (BM EA 571)	*s-n-wsrt*	man of the powerful one

A third type involves a pious statement in response to the child's birth:

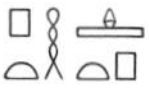	Ptahhotep (BM EA 584)	*ptḥ-ḥtp*	Ptah is content
	Inhuretnakht (BM EA 1783)	*inḥrt-nḫt*	Inhuret is strong

Loyalist names

Names which associate the individual with the king:

	Intef (BM EA 581)	*intf*	11th dynasty nomen
	Amenemhet (BM EA 587)	*imn-m-ḥꜣt*	12th dynasty nomen
	Nebipusenwosret (BM EA 101)	*nb(=i)-pw-snwsrt*	Senwosret is my lord

The birth names of the kings themselves accord with the standard naming conventions. Hence Amenemhet means 'Amun is in front', i.e. Amun is guiding the child's fortunes (compare with Senwosret above).

Kinship terms

Stelae emphasise family relationships by naming members of the deceased's family and household (often including servants and dependants). The living members are usually shown presenting offerings to the offering-table, thus eternalising the offering cult to the deceased owner in stone. By including the

various relatives and dependants on the monument of the deceased, these too enjoyed the benefits of being commemorated by figure and by name. Access to such monuments as funerary stelae was rather limited, mostly to those holding some form of élite position. The crucial relationship was that between the father and the eldest son: in social terms, this was the route of inheritance, providing family continuity; in cult terms, the eldest son was the chief celebrant for his father (as Horus was for Osiris).
Principal kinship terms:

 or 	*it*	father		*mwt*	mother
	*hi*	husband		*ḥmt*	wife
	*sn*	brother		*snt*	sister
	*s3*	son		*s3t*	daughter
	*3bt*	family, household			

Family members are often referred to as being 'beloved'.

Label before one of the sons of Khuenbik offering fowl:

BM EA 584: 
s3=f mry=f ptḥ-ḥtp
His son, his beloved, Ptahhotep

Sometimes, though, we find a more abbreviated writing.

Label before the first sons in the third row of BM EA 571:

BM EA 571: 
s3=f mry=f imny
His son, his beloved, Ameny

(In idiomatic English we might prefer 'his beloved son'.)

The parentage of the owner is usually introduced by one of the two following phrases:

 *ir-n* born of  *ms-n* born of

Literally, *ir-n* means 'whom X made' and *ms-n* means 'whom X bore'. Usually *ir-n* is used of both the father and mother, whereas *ms-n* is used of the mother alone. When the person this phrase is applied to is feminine, both, as usual, show a *-t* (before *n*).

The name and filiation of the wife of Ameny on BM EA 162 (see Exercise 8.5):

BM EA 162 

mdḥw mst-n ỉmny mȝʿt-ḫrw
Medhu born of Ameny, the justified

Properly speaking *ỉr-n* and *ms-n* are probably masculine relative forms – see §52 below. However, in this book we will stick to the distinctive transliteration using '-': *ỉr-n* and *ms-n*.

Exercises

5.1 Signs

 *ỉw*  *ḥs*  *ḥḳȝ*

 *nm*  *ḏȝ*

5.2 Words

Transliterate the following words written with these signs:

	....	favour, praise		....	friend
	....	boat-journey		....	proceed, go, set out
	....	ruler	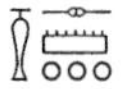	....	amethyst
	....	formal journey		....	wrong
	....	ferry			

nmtt is the word used for the formal and festal journeys of the god and the king. It is a collective term and not a plural (and hence does not require (*w*) in transliteration despite the presence of plural strokes).

5.3 Translation

Transliterate and translate the following sentences. Some were used in the text above and so give you the chance to work through these examples thoroughly. You may wish to consult §35 on the omission of the pronoun =*ỉ*.

a. Ikhernofret relates his role in the Mysteries of Osiris:

Berlin 1204, Line 18: 

(The verb *ỉr(ỉ)* 'to do' is used with a wide range of idiomatic meanings; here the sense is 'conduct'.)

b. The official Intef son of Senet proclaims his ethical behaviour:

BM EA 562, Line 10: 

c. Inhuretnakht extols his proper conduct as a responsible official:

BM EA 1783, Line 4: 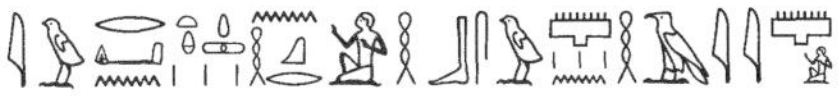

d. Another of Inhuretnakht's stated ethical acts (m added for clarity):

BM EA 1783, Lines 4-5: 

e. Ity notes his success and achievement:

BM EA 586, Line 2: 

For *e.* keep to a literal rendering of the Egyptian.

VOCABULARY

	*i3(w)*	the old		*iw3(w)*	cattle
	*iww*	the boatless		*ip*	inspect
	*wḥm*	repeat		*prt*	procession
	*mḫnt*	ferry		*nsw*	king
	*ḥ3y*	the naked		*ḥkr*	the hungry
	*ḫr*	before	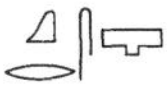	*krs*	bury
	*d3(i)*	ferry		*ḏs=i*	myself, my own

5.4 Study exercise: BM EA 1783

In this exercise, you can make a start on studying a more complex stela in the British Museum: BM EA 1783, the stela of the governor Inhuretnakht and his wife Hui from Nagʿ ed-Deir. The stela is shown on p. 74.

a. Transliterate and translate the offering formula at the top of the stela (Lines 1-2 ending with the word *ḏd* just before the end of Line 2), using the notes given.

b. Transliterate and translate the section starting at the beginning of Line 4 (we shall return to the section from the end of Line 2 to the end of Line 3 in Chapter 7).

The cemetery of Nagʿ ed-Deir, opposite modern Girga, was the cemetery for Thinis (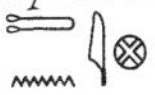 *ṯni*), the capital of the 8th Upper Egyptian nome (which also includes Abydos); *in-ḥrt* (Inhuret or Onuris) was its principal deity. Nagʿ ed-Deir was an important cemetery centre from Predynastic times to the 11th dynasty and the start of the Middle Kingdom, at which time Thinis seems to have been eclipsed by Abydos.

BM EA 1783
(carved and painted limestone; H. 66cm)

BM EA 1783 dates from the First Intermediate Period and is a classic example of the regional Nagʿ ed-Deir style of that period, both in terms of its artwork and the conventional phraseology of the inscription, which is orientated around the family and ethical behaviour.

Notes

i is a determinative of *prt-ḫrw*. See §26, p. 38

ii See Chapter 3 for the various titles of Inhuretnakht and the use of *ỉmꜣḫw* 'the revered one'. Be careful with the title at the start of line 2.

iii Self-presentation inscriptions are usually cast as a speech, and are introduced by *ḏd* 'who says' or *ḏd=f* 'he says'.

iv See §35 for the omission of the first person pronoun.

v *ḏs(=ỉ)* is used as the emphatic reflexive (as in 'I shall do that myself' or 'my own house').

vi Before *mḫnt* the preposition *m* 'in' has been omitted.

vii *ỉr(ỉ)* 'do, make' is used here in the sense of 'acquire' or possibly 'raise'.

VOCABULARY

	*ꜣbt*	family, household		*ỉww*	the boatless
	*ỉm(ꜣ)*	gracious, gentle		*ỉn-ḥrt-nḫt*	Inhuretnakht
	*ỉt*	father		*mwt*	mother
	*mr(ỉ)*	love		*mḫnt*	ferry
	*nb pt*	lord of the sky		*ḥꜣy*	the naked
	*ḥbsw*	clothes		*ḥs(ỉ)*	praise
	*ḥkr*	the hungry		*snw snwt*	siblings, brothers and sisters
	*kꜣ(w) 100*	100 bulls		*ḏꜣ(ỉ)*	ferry

The Family

c. Transliterate and translate the labels around the other family members. Hui has the following titles:

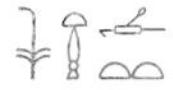	*ḫkrt nsw wʿtt*	sole lady in waiting		*ḥm(t)-nṯr ḥwt-ḥr*	priestess of Hathor

The form of the kinship expressions are alike, although some writings exhibit sharing of elements:

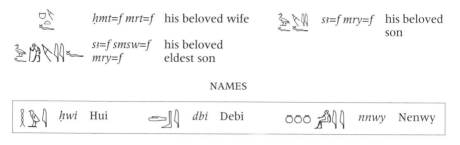

ḥmt=f mrt=f	his beloved wife
s3=f mry=f	his beloved son
s3=f smsw=f mry=f	his beloved eldest son

NAMES

ḥwi	Hui	*dbi*	Debi	*nnwy*	Nenwy

5.5 Study exercise: BM EA 571 (top)

The top section of the stela of Khu and her two husbands, shown on p. 77.

a. Translate the offering formulae above the two scenes.

VOCABULARY

m-r pr	steward, overseer of the estate	*s3-imn*	Saamun (name)
rḫ nsw mry nb=f	king's advisor beloved of his lord	*s3-ḥwt-ḥr*	Sahathor (name)
ḫw	Khu (name)	*nb imnt nfrt*	lord of the beautiful west

The second offering formula contains a different set of offerings:

mw	water	*mrḥt*	oil, unguent
ḥnḳt	beer	*snṯr*	incense

Festivals

The general word for a festival is *ḥb*: or — *ḥb* festival

The procession of Osiris to Poker: *ḏ3t nṯr r pḳr* the god's boat-journey to Poker

A number of particular or periodic festivals are often mentioned on stelae. The following is a list of the ones which appear on BM EA 571, arranged in the typical order in which they occur:

3bd	month festival	*?-nt*	half-month festival, i.e. full moon
w3g	the Wag-festival	*ḏḥwtt*	the Thoth-festival

The reading of the half-month festival is still unclear. An old suggestion to read *smdt* has problems. More recently, the suggestion has been made that the reading should be based around the number fifteen, as *mḏdint*.

The presence of the festivals on such stelae reflects the desire of the deceased to partake in the offerings made before the god in the temples on

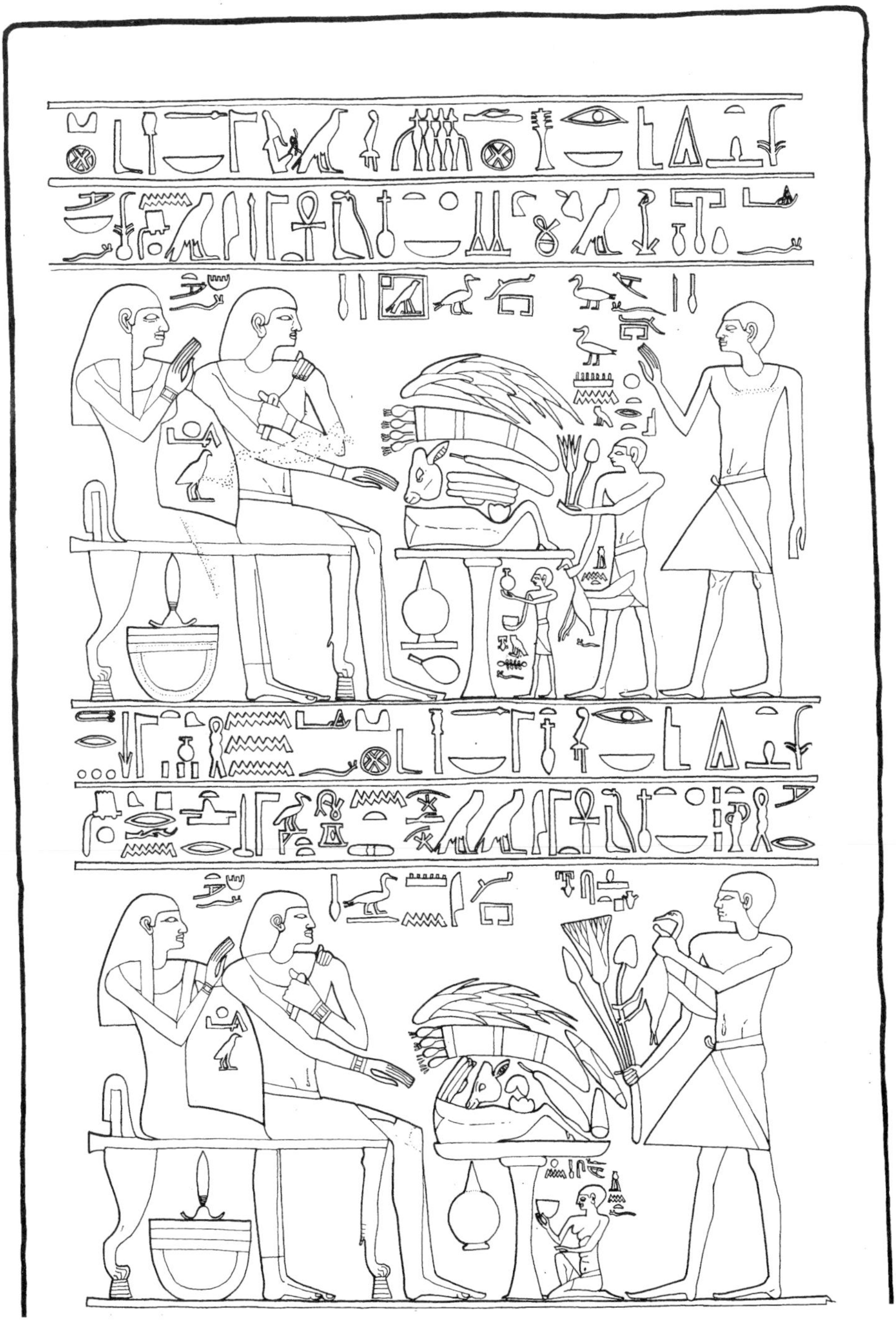

BM EA 571 (top)
(carved limestone; w. 51cm)

festival days; once the god had satisfied himself with them, they were passed on to the blessed dead. See the conclusion of the festival list on BM EA 162 in Exercise 8.5 for a further illustration of this point.

Offering bearers

b. Transliterate and translate the inscriptions accompanying the offering bearers in the two scenes. The inscriptions accompanying the two major offering bearers in the top scene fit the hieroglyphs around the figures. This can lead to unusual arrangements. They are given below in a conventional order:

accompanying the son	accompanying the overseer of the storehouse

VOCABULARY

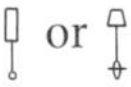	*wb3*	cup-bearer, butler		*m-r st*	overseer of the storehouse
	*m-s3=f*	Emsaf (name)		*ḫnms=f mry(=f)*	his beloved friend
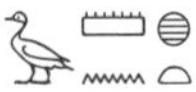	*s3-mnḫt*	Samenkhet (name)		*sḥtp-ib.*	Sehetepib (name, more fully Sehetepibre)

(Names ending with *m-s3=f* usually start with a god's name, as in *ḥr-m-s3=f* Horemsaf.)

5.6 Study exercise: BM EA 571 (bottom)

The bottom section of stela BM EA 571, shown on the following page, shows further family members and members of the household and estate staff.

a. Transliterate and translate the inscriptions. You may wish to make use of the Excursus on names and kinship.

b. Here are the names and titles in the scene. Some of the names are not transliterated. Transliterate them yourself:

NAMES AND TITLES

		Ameny		*s3t-mnṯw*	Satmentju
	*ṯ3w*	Tjau		*s3t-wsr(t)*	Satwosret
		Amenemhet		*bt*	Bet
	*ḫw*	Khu		*s3-ḥwt-ḥr*	Sahathor
	*ddt*	Dedet			Hetep
	*s-n-wsrt*	Senwosret		*ḥm-nṯr*	priest

OCCUPATIONS

ʿḳ(y)t	entering-maid (literally, 'the enterer')	*ḥrt-pr*	domestic
wbȝt	cup-bearer (fem.)	*sftw*	butcher
rḫty	washerman	*šmsw*	attendant

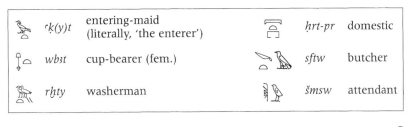

BM EA 571 (bottom)
(carved limestone; w. 51cm)

Chapter 6

Further aspects of description

In this chapter, we will look at how complex descriptions are presented, in particular continuing to the next point and noting other things going on at that time.

Now is a good time for you to start using the Egyptian-English vocabulary (starting on p. 151), when reading the examples in the text.

§38 Continuation

Descriptions are often presented as a series of connected episodes. In past descriptions, as we saw in Chapter 5, the first episode is introduced by an auxiliary such as *ỉw*, then described by a verb in the past tense made up of the *sḏm.n(=f)* form. A past description is continued on simply by carrying on with the *sḏm.n(=f)* without any further introductory auxiliary. In translating such a series, it is useful to translate the following *sḏm.n(=f)*s with 'and ...' (there is no separate word for 'and' in Egyptian), or to use commas or semi-colons, depending on English style:

The official Intef son of Senet proclaims his ethical behaviour in general terms:

BM EA 562, Lines 10-11:

ỉw ḳrs.n=ỉ ỉꜣ(w)
ḥbs.n=ỉ ḥꜣy

I buried the old
and I clothed the naked

Here the second past tense form  *ḥbs.n=ỉ* 'I clothed' carries on the description of Intef's ethical behaviour, rather than starting a new point. Notice how this gives a sense of shape and connection to episodes; for a clear example of the use of auxiliaries and *sḏm.n(=f)*s to give shape to description, see Exercise 6.5 below.

Sometimes elements are shared, just as in the English translation:

Inhuretnakht is extolling his proper conduct as a responsible official:

BM EA 1783, Line 4:

ỉw rdỉ.n(=ỉ) t n ḥḳr
ḥbs(w) n ḥꜣy

I gave bread to the hungry
and clothes to the naked

(…) *rdi.n(=i)* 'I gave' is shared: 'I gave bread to the hungry and (I gave) clothes to the naked'.

Ity notes his success and achievement:

BM EA 586, Line 2:

iw wḥm.n(=i) ḥst ḫr nsw
sꜥꜣ ib(=i) r it(w)(=i) ḫprw r-ḥꜣt=i

I repeated favour before the king
and advanced my heart further than my forefathers who existed before me

Notes

i …*.n(=i)* 'I ..-(e)d' is shared: 'I repeated favour ... and (I) advance(d) my heart'.
ii *r* 'to, in relation to' sometimes has the sense of 'more than'.
iii *ḫprw* 'who existed' is a participle (see Chapter 7).

§39 Negation

The negative of the past ('I did not do that') is made up of the negative word … *n* followed by *sḏm(=f)* (it is not, as we might expect, formed by *n sḏm.n(=f)*!):

Following on immediately from his statement of positive ethical virtues (see above), Intef adds:

BM EA 562, Line 11:

n ir(=i) iwit r rmṯ
I did not do wrong against people (or: I did no wrong ...)

This negation also occurred in the opening scene to this book (notice the slightly stronger translation with 'never'):

Above the man roasting a goose:

Meir III, pl. 23:

n mꜣ=i mity srw pn
I have never seen the like of this goose

Sometimes the negation is written (rather confusingly!) with … .

The official Key notes his ethical virtues:

BM EA 558, Line 5: *n ḏws(=ỉ) s n ḥry-tp=f*
I did not denounce a man to his superior

The negative word 𓂜 *n* does not go with auxiliaries such as *ỉw* (see §34). Therefore a statement beginning with 𓂜 *n* can be used to start a new episode, or just as easily to carry on a series of connected episodes (see §38).

§40 Making someone do something (for use with Exercise 6.5)
Causation, the notion of 'making someone do something', is expressed in the following way in Egyptian: the verb *rdỉ* 'give, place' is used with the sense of 'causing' and is followed by another verb. *rdỉ* appears in whatever form is suitable (in the example below it appears in the past tense *sḏm.n(=f)* form) whilst the other verb appears in a fixed form (as it happens, the other verb appears in the future *sḏm(=f)*, for which see Chapter 8; however, this is not important at this point):

After the festivities are over, Ikhernofret has the image of the god placed back in the bark (see Exercise 6.5 for the general context of this example):

Berlin 1204, Lines 21-22: ***dỉ**.n=ỉ wḏꜣ=f r-ẖnw wrt*
I **had** him proceed inside the great bark
(literally, 'I caused that he proceed inside the great bark')

It may help to think of this as 'placing someone in the position to do something' or 'giving someone the opportunity to do something'; hence the example would mean: 'I put him (in the position) to proceed inside the great bark' or 'I facilitated his proceeding into the great bark'. The precise meaning can range from nuances of compulsion ('make someone do something') to permission ('allow/let someone to do something') and guidance ('have someone do something').

§41 Dependent pronouns
The second set of pronouns are the *dependent pronouns* (see Reference table, p. 149):

I	 or 	*-wỉ* or *-w(ỉ)*	he/it	 or 	*-sw*
you	 or 	*-ṯw* or *-tw*	she/it	 or 	*-sy* or *-s(y)*

The major usage of the dependent pronouns are as the objects of verbs (typically the person or thing to which the verbal action is applied):

Tjetji records that, after Intef II died, he served the new king Intef III:

BM EA 614, Line 13:
ỉw šms.n(=ỉ) **-sw** *r s(w)t=f nbt nfrt nt sḫmḫ-ỉb*
I followed **him** to all his perfect places of delight
(i.e. wherever the king wanted to go)

Notice that the suffix pronouns serve as subjects of the verb (see §§33 and 36) and dependent pronouns as objects of the verb.

The dependent pronouns display an important feature of word ordering: the dependent pronouns attach to and directly follow the verb and so *precede* any nouns:

The official Semti refers to his early favour at court:

BM EA 574, Lines 2-3:
ỉw dỉ.n -wỉ ḥm=f r rdwy=f m nḫnt(=ỉ)
His person (i.e. the king) placed me at his feet in my youth

If you look carefully at this example, then *-wỉ* is a dependent pronoun and therefore should be the object of the verb (someone must have placed **me**) and so the sentence must mean that the king placed me at his feet, despite the order of the words. This sentence cannot mean: 'I placed the king at his feet in my youth' (for 'I' to be the subject, this would require the suffix pronoun *=ỉ*) and in any case such a sentence scarcely makes much sense.

§42 The present tense

The monuments discussed in this book do not include many inscriptions cast in the present tense. However, for your information, and to allow us to cover one inscription we would otherwise have shown you but not equipped you to read, we will briefly note the present tense forms.

Middle Kingdom Egyptian distinguishes, just as English does, between a *general present* (usually expressing habit – She **goes** to visit her friend every week' – or things which just generally are – 'two and two **make** four') and *a specific or ongoing present* ('She **is leaving** right now'). In Middle Egyptian these have the following form (using *sḏm* to label the form and the weak verb *ỉr(ỉ)* to exemplify it):

GENERAL PRESENT *sḏm=f*	SPECIFIC PRESENT *ḥr sḏm*
 *ỉr=f* he does	 *ḥr ỉrt* (he) is doing

In the specific present, the verb appears after *ḥr* in the infinitive form discussed in Chapter 4. For a full list of forms, see the Reference tables on p. 145.

Both tenses have a fondness for the auxiliary  *ỉw* introduced in §34 as illustrated by the examples below. They also share the same intricacies of usage as their English equivalents (for example, in Egyptian, as in English, verbs of state and condition prefer the general present to the specific present even when referring to things going on now: 'I know the answer now', not 'I am knowing the answer now'):

a. sḏm(=f)

To the left of the main offering formula inscription on BM EA 587:

BM EA 587:

ỉw wꜥb ḫꜣ m t ḥnḳt snṯr mrḥt
The thousand(s) of bread, beer, incense and oil are pure

b. ḥr sḏm

An example of this construction occurred in the first inscription shown to you in this book:

Above the man roasting a goose:

Meir III, pl. 23:

ỉw=ỉ ḥr mꜥḳ ḏr pꜣt
I have been roasting since the beginning of time

Egyptian, like many languages, concentrates on the fact that the subject is continuing to roast despite the long time he has been doing it: 'I am still roasting and have been since the beginning of time'.

§43 Other things going on (advanced notes for use with Exercise 6.5)
However, there is one use of the present tense which will be useful when you study Exercise 6.5. In past description, as we have seen, the past events are described by using the past tense *sḏm.n(=f)* form. By stringing together a present *sḏm(=f)* form or *ḥr sḏm* form after a past *sḏm.n(=f)*, Egyptian expresses the notion of something else going on at the same time as that event expressed by the *sḏm.n(=f)* form (something else current or present at that time):

Ikhernofret relates his activities during the performance of the Mysteries of Osiris:

Berlin 1204, Line 17:

ỉw ỉr.n=ỉ prt wp-wꜣwt ***wḏꜣ=f*** *r nḏ ỉt=f*
I conducted the procession of Wepwawet
when he set out to protect his father

Notes

i  *ỉr(ỉ)* literally, 'do, make', here with the sense of leading or conducting.

ii *r nḏ* preposition + infinitive 'to protect'.

Notice that there is no Egyptian word for 'when', 'while', 'as' in these usages, although the appropriate English word may be needed in translation. In English, the notion of 'going on at the same time' is expressed by connecting words such as 'as', 'whilst', 'when'. In Egyptian it is the verb itself which expresses this by appearing in a present tense form (present or going on at that time). Indeed, you may have noticed that whereas in English connections are shown by words such as 'and' and 'as', in Egyptian the same meaning is achieved by stringing together different tenses such as *sḏm.n(=f)* and *sḏm(=f)* and letting the verbs do the work.

Exercises

6.1 Signs

2-consonant and 3-consonant signs:

	*mi͗*		*ḏr*		*ḫsf*
	*nḏ*		*ḳd*		*šms*

6.2 Words

Transliterate the following words written with these signs:

	....	since		....	like, as
	....	protect, save		....	drive away, repel
	....	the like, peer, equal		....	night of vigil
	....	sail		....	follow

6.3 Translation

Transliterate and translate the following (see §35 on omission of =*i͗* 'I').

The first one repeats examples from the chapter above and is written here without any breaks (as in the original inscription):

a. The official Intef son of Senet proclaims his ethical behaviour in general terms:

BM EA 562,
Lines 10-11: 

b. Hekaib asserts his ethical behaviour:

BM EA 1671,
Lines 4-5: 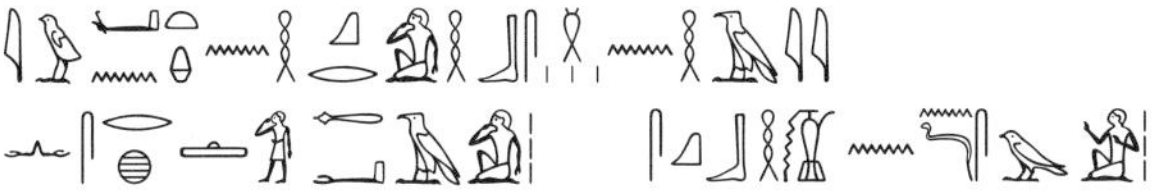

This First Intermediate Period stela shows a number of idiosyncracies in the spelling, such as the form of *di͗* ( instead of ) and the form of the determinative for 'clothes'.

The final example is slightly more complex and is written in the right-to-left order of the original:

c. Tjetji describes his advancement by king Intef II:

BM EA 614, Lines 4-5:

Notes

i -*w* is written for -*wỉ*.

ii Read *dỉ.n=f -w(ỉ)* in clause 3.

iii Also read *ꜥḥ=f n wꜥꜥw*.

6.4 Translation

It has been a long time coming, but you are now in a position to read for yourself the speech of the man roasting the goose, which we used to begin this book. This is shown again below.

Notes

i On suffix pronouns, see §33 and §36.

ii On the *ḥr* + infinitive tense, see §42.

iii On negation, see §39.

VOCABULARY

	*ỉwỉt*	wrong		*ꜥꜣ(w)*	the great
	*ꜥḥ*	palace		*wꜥꜥw*	privacy
	*pꜣt*	the beginning of time		*pn*	this
	*mꜥḳ*	roast		*mity*	equal
	*nḏs(w)*	ordinary folk, the lowly		*rmṯ*	people
	*ḥbs*	clothe (verb)		*ḥry-tp*	superior, chief

VOCABULARY (CONTINUED)

	*sꜥꜣ*	advance, promote		*srw*	goose
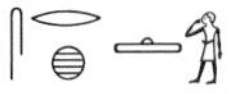	*srḫ*	complain about, accuse	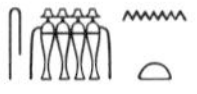	*sḫnt*	augment, promote
	*sḳbḥ*	put (someone) at ease		*st*	place, position, status
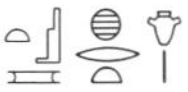	*st ḥrt-ỉb*	confidence		*ḏr*	since

6.5 Study exercise: The Osiris Mysteries at Abydos

The celebration of the Mysteries of Osiris at Abydos was clearly one of the major festivals of Middle Kingdom Egypt. The festival centred around the burial and rejuvenation of Osiris, with its promise of burial and rejuvenation for the blessed dead. Indeed, as discussed in Chapter 4, a number of the élite erected stelae or cenotaphs in the area bordering the route to ensure their eternal participation in the rites.

The festival itself seems to have comprised five parts:

1 The first procession led by Wepwawet and culminating in combat against the enemies of Osiris. This seems to have been a celebration of kingship with the repelling of the forces of chaos and disorder (possibly reflecting the threat of disorder at the death of the old king Osiris – see p. 41 for the mythological account).

2 The great procession of Osiris himself. This seems to have been the start of the burial procession of Osiris as the dead king, when he was equipped and prepared for burial. Osiris here appeared in his form of Khentyimentu 'the one who is foremost of the westerners' and was taken out from the temple through the surrounding cemetery site.

3 The god's boat-journey to Poker. The god was conveyed in the great bark out into the desert to his supposed tomb at Poker (probably the tomb of King Djer of the First Dynasty at Umm el-Qaꜥab).

4 A night of vigil in which the god was rejuvenated as Wenennefer (see p. 42), including the Haker-festivities and a slaughter of the enemies of Osiris at Nedyet (the mythological place of his death). Unfortunately, this remains the most secretive and elusive part of the mysteries, though later accounts mention that Osiris was crowned with the crown of justification ( *mꜣꜥ-ḫrw*) and transfigured or enspirited ( *sꜣḫ*).

5 The return journey to Abydos among general rejoicing and the re-entry of the god into his temple.

The stela of the Treasurer Ikhernofret, now in Berlin, is one of the principal sources for the Osiris Mysteries. Ikhernofret was sent to Abydos by

Senwosret III to repair the image of the god and to perform the necessary ritual acts. He subsequently erected a stela in which he recounts how he organised the festival (an account which draws on previous versions given by earlier generations of officials sent by the Middle Kingdom kings to Abydos).

a. Transliterate and translate the following sections from the stela of Ikhernofret:

There follows a brief description of the manner in which Ikhernofret equipped the bark and put the proper regalia on the god, then:

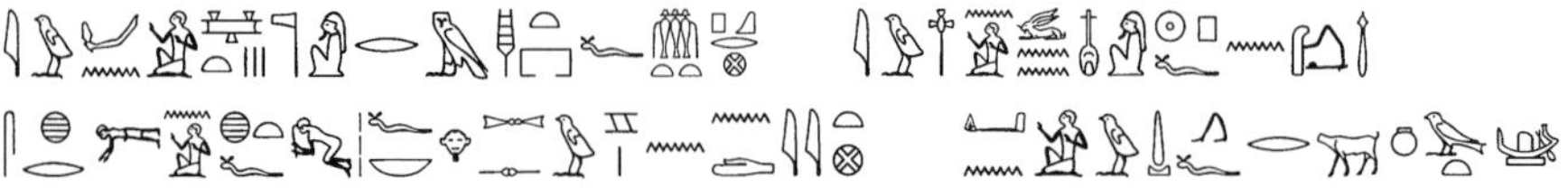

The stela is unfortunately silent on the most mysterious features of the festivities such as the night of vigil and the Haker-festivities (compare with BM EA 567 in Study Exercise 8.3). There follows a description of the rejoicing along the route back, ending with the boat arriving at Abydos, then:

Notes

i *r nḏ* preposition + infinitive, translate 'to protect'. On the writing of *ỉt*, 'father', see Exercise 2.5: read here *ỉt=f* 'his father'.

ii You may find §43 helpful in translating *wḏꜣ=f* and *šms=ỉ*.

iii You may find §27 on the direct and indirect genitive helpful.

iv *ḏsr* as an adjective means 'sacred' (in *tꜣ ḏsr* 'sacred land') and as a verb means 'to clear (something) out'; in this text the verb is deliberately chosen to mark the transition of the festival from the public view to the hidden mysteries to take place at the tomb, and this happens once the procession has passed through *tꜣ ḏsr*.

v See §40 on *dỉ.n=ỉ* followed by a verb to express causation.

vi *hrw pf* 'that day', translate '(on) that day ...'

vii The bark of Osiris is called the Neshmet-bark (*nšmt*) or else is simply referred to as the great bark (*wrt*); both are feminine words and are refered to by the feminine pronoun *=s* 'it' in *ỉn.n=s* 'it brought' (for *ỉn(ỉ)* 'bring', see p.44). See the reference table on suffix pronouns on p. 148.

VOCABULARY

(for other words, see Egyptian-English Vocabulary, beginning on p. 151)

ỉt	father	*ꜥḥ*	palace, temple
ꜥḥꜣ	fight, fighting	*wꜣ(w)t*	ways, roads
wnn-nfr	Wenennefer (name of Osiris)	*wrt*	the great bark
wḏꜣ	proceed, go, set out	*pf*	that
pḳr	Poker	*mꜥḥꜥt*	tomb, often cenotaph
nmtt	journey	*nšmt*	Neshmet-bark
nṯr	god	*ndyt*	Nedyet
nḏ	protect, save	*hrw*	day
ḥr	(up)on, at	*ḫft(w)*	enemies
ḫntt	(which is) at the forefront of	*ḫsf*	drive away, repel
ẖnw	inside	*sbỉ(w)*	rebels, enemies
sḫr	fell, overturn	*sḳd(ỉ)*	sail, travel
šms	follow	*ṯsw*	(sand)bank
dpt-nṯr	the god's boat	*ḏsr*	separate, clear

EXTRA VOCABULARY

hꜣkr	the Haker-festivities	*sḏrt*	night of vigil

b. Look at the episodes in this section from the stela of Ikhernofret and examine how *ỉw* and the past tense *sḏm.n(=f)* form are used to give shape to the passage. As a guide, note that in most instances, the auxiliary *ỉw* is followed not by one but by two or three past-tense verbs; only in the sentence beginning *ỉw ḏsr.n=ỉ* is *ỉw* followed by a single verb. How does your grammatical account correlate with the different sections of the festival?

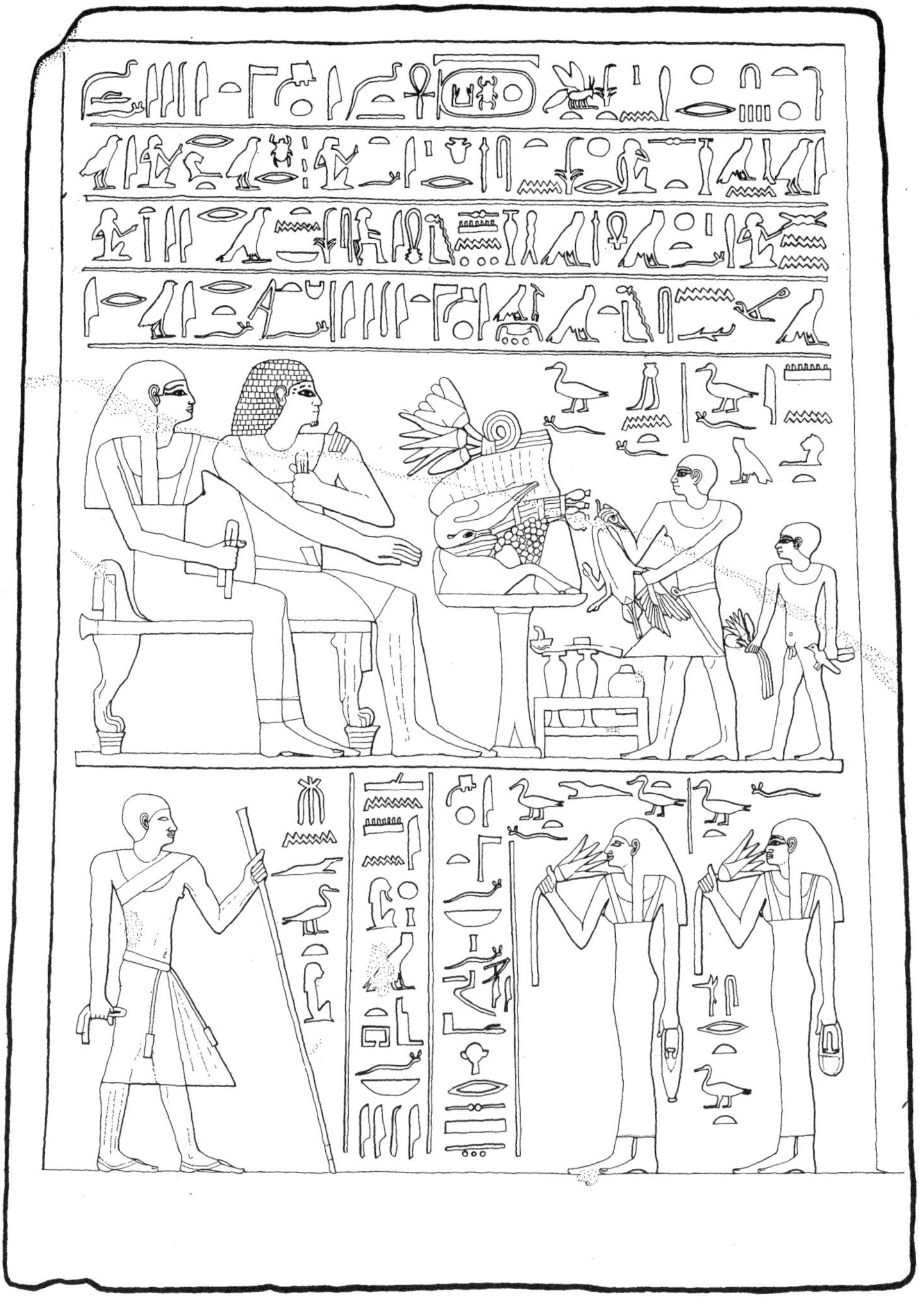

BM EA 586
(carved and painted limestone; H. 63.5cm)

6.6 Study exercise: BM EA 586

a. The stela on p. 90 is by no means an easy text, but with the help of the following notes, have a go at transliterating and translating the top section of this stela or use the key on p. 170 to work through it.

Notes

i On dating and the titles of the king, see §§17-19. The king's cartouche is surmounted by the sky hieroglyph, which is not read.

ii *wḥm ḥst* 'to repeat favour' with *wḥm* in the *sḏm.n(=f)* form. On the omission of *=ỉ* 'I', see §35.

iii *sꜥꜣ* 'to advance' (one's position, here 'heart') literally, 'to make great'. The full form would have been *sꜥꜣ.n=ỉ*, see §38 on coordination and sharing. *r* has the sense here of 'more than'.

iv *ḫprw* 'who existed' is a participle (see Chapter 7 for discussion).

v The section beginning *ỉw ṯs.n* is another example of coordination, here dealing with the king's gift of a great seal (*ḫtm ꜥꜣ*) and a staff (*ꜣryt*) to Ity. *ṯs(ỉ)* lit. 'to tie on', is used for the seal which the king tied around Ity's neck, but this precise meaning does not really go with the decorated staff which Ity was also given, so translate 'assign (to)'.

vi *mỉ šps-nsw nb* 'just like any dignitary of the king' (which you might wish to put in brackets) goes with the first gift (the seal), and contrasts with the special gift of the staff (with which Ity is depicted in the lower scene). *šps-nsw* is a conventional designation.

vii *swꜥbt* is a participle with feminine agreement with *ꜣryt* 'staff', translate '(which was) decorated'. See Chapter 7.

viii *ỉt-nṯr* 'god's father'. In the Middle Kingdom, this seems to have been a title bestowing high rank and favour on an official, typically for performing special commissions for the king to do with the cult of the gods, and also legitimating him for this task. Perhaps here the title is directly connected to the episode of the king's assignment of the great seal and a staff to Ity.

ix The text ends abruptly with the names of Ity and Iuri. The wife's name is separated off by a vertical bar.

VOCABULARY

	*ꜣryt*	staff		*ỉwrỉ*	Iuri (name)
	*ỉb*	heart		*ỉt(w)*	(fore-) fathers
 or	*ỉt-nṯr*	god's father		*ỉty*	Ity (name)
	*wḥm*	repeat		*nsw*	king

VOCABULARY (CONTINUED)

	*r-ḥ3t*	before		*hbny*	ebony
	*ḥmt=f mrt=f*	his beloved wife		*ḥst*	favour
	*ḥsmn*	amethyst		*ḫpr*	come into being, exist
	*ḫpr-k3-rꜥ*	Kheperkare (Senwosret I)		*ḫr*	before
	*ḫtm*	seal		*sꜥ3*	advance
	*swꜥb*	decorate		*šps-nsw*	dignitary of the king
	ṯs(i)	tie, knot		*ḏꜥm*	electrum

The family

b. Transliterate and translate the labels above the sons and daughters of Ity.

VOCABULARY: NAMES

	*imn-m-ḥ3t*	Amenemhet		*int=f*	Intef
	*s3t-wsrt*	Satwosret		*s3t-sbk*	Satsobek

You will be asked to study the inscription from the bottom scene at the end of Chapter 7.

Chapter 7

Characterisation

This chapter concentrates on the elaborate epithets which abound on stelae, particularly epithets characterising the owner as having lived an ethical life or having performed well in royal service. This will also allow us to introduce you to another extremely common Egyptian verb-form – the participle. To start with, however, we need to return to adjectives.

§44 Adjectives

You have already been introduced to adjectives in §10. In Egyptian, these follow and agree with the noun they describe. If the noun is feminine and ends in *-t*, the adjective will also end in *-t*. To wrap up this topic properly, the full list of endings are:

SG. MSC.		no special ending		*nfr*
SG. FEM.		*-t*	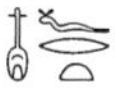	*nfrt*
PL. MSC.		*-w* or ø		*nfr(w)*
PL. FEM.		*-t*	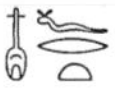	*nfrt*

(The plural can be written with or without the plural strokes ı ı ı; moreover, the *-w* of the masculine plural agreement is often omitted in writing, leaving no ending at all – this is indicated by the symbol ø in the table above.)

Compare the following examples showing feminine singular agreement and masculine plural agreement:

Ikhernofret relates his role in the Mysteries of Osiris:

Berlin 1204, Line 18: *iw ir.n=i prt* ***ꜥ3t***
I conducted the **great** procession

The top part of BM EA 101 has Nebipusenwosret adoring the gods. Behind the figure of Nebipusenwosret:

BM EA 101: 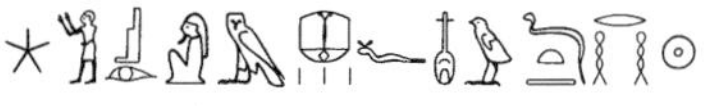

dwꜣ ꜣsỉr m ḥb(w)=f ***nfrw*** *ḏt r nḥḥ*
Adoring Osiris in his **wonderful** festivals enduringly and repeatedly

§45 Adjectives used as nouns

Adjectives are typically used to describe other words, but they can be used on their own to mean 'a person/people with that particular quality'. For example, in English 'I am an **Egyptian**', means 'I am an **Egyptian person**' (not a soldier, or a donkey, or anything else!); compare also English expressions such as the 'the rich' and 'the poor'. In Egyptian this is rather common:

The official Intef, son of Senet, proclaims his ethical behaviour in general terms:

BM EA 562, Lines 10-11:

ỉw ḳrs.n=ỉ ***ỉꜣ(w)*** *ḥbs.n=ỉ* ***ḥꜣy***
I buried **the old** and I clothed **the naked**

However, in Egyptian, the adjective can be singular with the meaning 'a rich one/(some)one rich', whereas English prefers to add a rather general word such as 'someone' (so *ḥꜣy* probably means more accurately 'someone naked' or 'the naked one').

If the idea is indefinite, abstract or general: 'anything good' or 'what is good', the feminine form of the adjective is used:

	*nfrt*	good (n.) 'what is good'	from	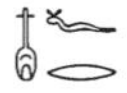	*nfr*	good, perfect
	*bỉnt*	evil (n.) 'what is bad'	from		*bỉn*	bad

Key proclaims his own ethical behaviour:

BM EA 558, Line 4:

ỉnk ḏd nfrt
I was one who said **what is good**

Notes

i For *ỉnk* , see §49 below.

ii *ḏd* is a participle meaning 'one who said', see §§48 and 49.

The meaning of the feminine form of the adjective as 'what is good' is similar to the meaning of the relative form mentioned in §37.

§46 Participles

The participles are special forms of the verb which have many of the qualities of an adjective, particularly because they can be used to qualify nouns.

There are two groups of participles: the present participle has the meaning '(one) who does something'; the past participle has the meaning '(one) who did something'. The forms of the participles in different verb classes are as follows:

	PRESENT OR INCOMPLETE			PAST OR COMPLETE		
STRONG		*sḏm*	(one) who hears		*sḏm*	(one) who heard
DOUBLING		*m33*	(one) who sees		*m3*	(one) who saw
WEAK		*mrr*	(one) who loves		*mr*	(one) who loved
EXTRA WEAK		*dd* (no *r*)	(one) who gives		*rdì* (with *r*)	(one) who gave

(Participles also sometimes have a -*w* ending.)

Basically, any verb other than a strong verb has a doubled consonant in the present participle but not in the past participle. In the case of strong verbs, however, it is not possible to tell the two apart on the basis of their forms alone. As you will see in the examples below, there is no need in Egyptian for a separate word meaning 'who' (or 'which' or 'what') since this is an integral part of the meaning of the Egyptian participle verb-form.

§47 Participles and epithets

Since a participle behaves a lot like an adjective, it is often used to qualify a noun. For example, participles are commonly used in the epithets characterising an official:

The stela of Ameny identifies his subordinate, Sahathor, with the epithet:

BM EA 162, Central column: *b3k=f m3ʿ n st-ìb=f* ***ìrr*** *ḥsst=f rʿ nb*

His true servant of his affection, **who does** what he favours every day

(*ḥsst=f* 'what he favours' is a present relative form, see §52 below. For the writing of *ìrr*, see Ex. 7.3 below.)

In the first part of this example both  *m3ʿ* 'true' and  *n st-ìb=f* 'of his affection' help to characterise  *b3k=f* 'his servant'. Similarly in the second half of the example,  *ìrr* is the present participle ('who does') and is also used to elaborate the character of  *b3k=f* 'his servant'.

Just like an adjective, a participle must agree with the noun it describes and so will end with -*t* if the noun is feminine:

Before the figure of Medehu, the wife of Ameny:

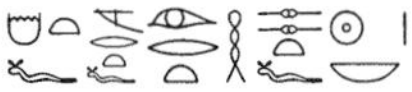

BM EA 162, Left column: *ḥmt=f mrt=f* ***ỉrrt*** *ḥsst=f rꜥ nb*
His wife, beloved of him, **who does** what he favours every day

In this example, *ỉrrt* ('who does') agrees with *ḥmt* 'wife'; for *mrt* 'beloved', see §50, below.

Alternatively, a participle may show an extra -*w* with masculine plurals:

Ity asserts that he advanced himself more than:

BM EA 586, Line 2: *ỉt(w)=ỉ* ***ḫprw*** *r-ḥꜣt=ỉ*
my (fore-)fathers who **existed** before me

§48 Participles as nouns

Again, like adjectives, participles can be used on their own to mean 'a person who does something' or more succinctly 'one who does something'. For example, BM EA 614 (the stela of Tjetji) introduces Tjetji himself with a long list of his titles and epithets, including:

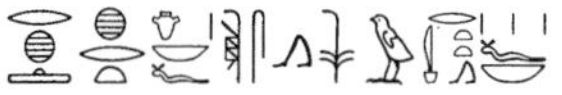

BM EA 614, Line 1: *rḫ ḫrt-ib nb=f*
šms -sw r nmtt=f nb
one who knows the desire of his lord,
one who follows him at all his journeys

(For vocabulary, see p. 106.)

In this example, *rḫ* and *šms* are participles used on their own to mean '(a person) who knows' and '(a person) who follows'.

Incidentally, the participle is the form used in the name of Wepwawet, 'the one who opens the ways' (compare this with his role in the Osiris Mysteries studied in Exercise 6.5):

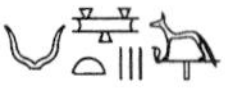 *wp-wꜣwt* Wepwawet

(Participles used on their own sometimes translate well as an English agentive noun ending in '-er', here 'the opener of the ways'.)

§49 Characterisation with *ỉnk*

This construction is typically used to characterise someone as the type of person with certain qualities or attributes; in effect, it answers the question 'what was I like?', 'who was I?', focusing on ethical behaviour and success and achievement:

The self-presentation section of the stela of Hekaib begins in the following way:

BM EA 1671, Line 1: *ỉnk nḏs ỉḳr*
I was an astute individual

ỉnk is the 'I'-form (first person) of a third and last type of pronoun, called the *independent pronoun* because it can come at the beginning of a statement:

 or  *ỉnk* I — Independent pronoun, written with the D33 pot, read here as *ỉn*.

Notice that in this example there is no word for 'was' in this construction (the statement could also be translated in the present tense, i.e. 'I am an astute individual', but here the past tense seems appropriate to the idea of an official looking back over a life presented as now ended).

It is not unusual to find the use of qualifying expressions such as participles:

The self-presentation of Hekaib continues:

BM EA 1671, Line 1: *ỉnk nḏs ỉḳr*
ḏd *m r=f*
I was an astute individual,
who spoke with his (own) mouth

The owner is referred to the second time in the third person:  *=f*, moving from the specific individual to a generalized social characterisation by characterising the first person 'I' (specific individual) in generalized third person terms ('one who spoke with his own mouth').

In this example, the adjective (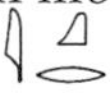 *ỉḳr* 'astute') and the participle ( *ḏd* 'who spoke') both qualify  *nḏs*. Often, however, *ỉnk* is followed by a participle used on its own, to create a statement which means 'I was someone who did' (when using the past participle):

The official Key makes a common statement about appropriate behaviour:

BM EA 558, Line 4: *ỉnk* ***ḏd*** *nfrt*
I was **one who said** what is good

This *characterisation* construction tells us about what he was like. It does not mean 'I said what is good' – this would be a description, using the past tense *sḏm.n(=f)* form, and would tell us about what he did, rather than what he was like:

A made-up example to illustrate the point in the text:

ỉw ***ḏd.n****=ỉ nfrt*
I **said** what is good

The two constructions differ clearly in form and also in meaning, just as their English translations do.

§50 Passive participles

Participles can either be active ('one who loved') or passive ('one who was (be)loved'). Unfortunately, the passive participles do not usually have a distinctive writing in Egyptian. However, the most common examples in our inscriptions concern the verbs *mr(ỉ)* 'love' and *ḥs(ỉ)* 'favour' which, as weak verbs, do sometimes show a distinctive *–y* ending in the past passive participle. Since this is a rather common usage, we will discuss the point in some detail:

Inhuretnakht declares his status within his family:

BM EA 1783, Lines 2-3:

ỉnk ***mry n*** *ỉt=f*
I was **one beloved** of his father

In such a usage, the passive participle is often followed by the genitive 'of', either the indirect genitive (as in the last example) or the direct genitive:

Tjetji declares his status in relation to the king:

BM EA 614, Line 3:

ỉnk ***mry*** *nb=f*
I was **one beloved** of his lord

The passive participle may even be followed by a suffix pronoun:

The stela of Tjetji continues:

BM EA 614, Line 3:

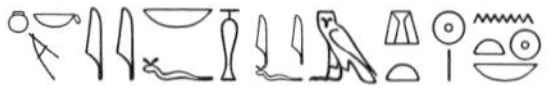

ỉnk mry nb=f
ḥsy=f *m ẖrt-hrw nt rꜥ -nb*

I was one beloved of his lord
and **favoured of him** (or, 'his favoured one')
in the course of every day

In expressions of familial affection,  *mr(ỉ)* sometimes occurs in the present/incomplete participle form 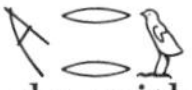 *mrrw*. The reason for this is still much discussed and may have to do with the presence of the following plural genitive expression. However, a much easier way to understand this in the next example is to note that that the previous generation (the owner's mother and father) take the past passive participle, whereas his siblings (i.e. the present generation from his point of view) take the present passive participle:

Inhuretnakht's full declaration of his status within his family (this completes Study Exercise 5.4):

BM EA 1783, Lines 2-3:

ỉnk mry n ỉt=f ḥsy n mwt=f mrrw snw=f snwt=f ỉm(ꜣ) n ꜣbt=f
I was one beloved of his father, praised of his mother, beloved of his siblings, and one gracious of/to his household

(For the phrase *snw=f snwt=f*, see p. 75.)

As an alternative, *mrrw* might be translated as a masculine relative form – see §52 below – and the translation reshaped: 'one whom his siblings love and one gracious to his household'.

Finally, you have already encountered the past passive usage on a number of occasions in various labels of filiation. A particularly good example occurs on BM EA 584, to be studied in Chapter 8:

Label before one of the sons of Khuenbik offering fowl:

BM EA 584:

sꜣ=f mry=f ptḥ-ḥtp
His son, his beloved, Ptahhotep

Often, though, we find a more abbreviated writing:

Label before the first sons in the third row of BM EA 571:

BM EA 571:

sꜣ=f mry=f ỉmny
His son, his beloved, Ameny

(In idiomatic English we might prefer 'his beloved son'.)

§51 *ỉn* + noun + participle

The participles are also used in a construction introduced by *ỉn*: *ỉn* + noun + participle 'it is so-and-so who did'. Like its English equivalent, this construction highlights the person who performs an action. It occurs quite commonly in a dedication formula which identifies the donor of a stela:

The label above Niptahkau on the stela dedicated to his father Khuenbik (see Chapter 8, pp. 122-3):

BM EA 584: *ỉn sꜣ=f sꜥnḫ rn=f m-r ỉḳdw(w) n-ptḥ-kꜣw*
It is his son who made his name live (on), the overseer of builders Niptahkau

§52 Relative forms again

In §37 above we introduced you to the past relative form. The relative form is in fact similar in usage to the participle. First of all, here is a table of the forms of the relative forms in the present and the past. As with the previous section on the relative form §37, we shall exhibit the form with a *-t* (although, as you will see, this is actually the *-t* of feminine agreement):

	PRESENT OR INCOMPLETE		
STRONG		*sḏmt=f*	what he hears
DOUBLING		*mꜣꜣt=f*	what he sees
WEAK		*mrrt=f*	what he loves
EXTRA WEAK		*ddt=f*	what he gives
	PAST OR COMPLETE		
STRONG		*sḏmt.n=f*	what he heard
DOUBLING		*mꜣt.n=f*	what he saw
WEAK		*mrt.n=f*	what he loved
EXTRA WEAK		*rdỉt.n=f*	what he gave

(Compare with the forms of the participles in §46 above.)

In particular, like participles, relative forms display certain adjectival qualities. Thus they agree with the noun they accompany, for example taking a *-t* when going with feminine words. A good example occurs in the offering formula:

The offering formula in BM EA 558:

BM EA 558, Line 2:	*ḫt -nbt nfr(t) wꜥb(t)* ***ꜥnḫt*** *nṯr ỉm* everything good and pure on **which** a god **lives**

Also, just like adjectives, the relative forms show this helpful extra ⏓ *-t* when used on their own with the meaning '**what** someone does/did':

The stela of Ameny identifies his subordinate, Sahathor, with the epithet:

BM EA 162, Central column:	*bꜣk=f mꜣꜥ n st-ỉb=f* *ỉrr* ***ḥsst=f*** *rꜥ nb* His true servant of his affection, who does **what he favours** every day

Masculine relative forms do not show such a ⏓ *-t* and thus are harder to spot. Fortunately they are also fairly uncommon and need not concern us in this book. As noted in Chapter 5, p. 71, the filiation expressions for males *ỉr-n* and *ms-n* may well be examples of masculine relative forms.

Excursus: Middle Kingdom titles

In Chapter 3, various titles were introduced to provide you with a resource for your reading. In these notes, the titles are gathered together according to their function, to provide another convenient reference resource (the list includes some titles from other stelae in the British Museum).

General terms

Generic terms for office holding and status amongst the élite include the following:

	*ỉꜣt*	office		*sr*	official
	*bꜣk*	servant		*nḏs*	individual

The term *ỉꜣt* is the general term for a regular office or function. Such an office brought status, position and power, and also wealth through its attached estate (*pr*). The term *bꜣk* 'servant' was often used as a means of stressing the dependent relationship of one person on another and could be used of people who otherwise had high status. *nḏs* 'individual' was often used, particularly in the First Intermediate Period, for someone of high status who did not hold an official position.

The palace and the king

The 'palace' was an itinerant community gathered round the king, who, as well as residing at a central residential and administrative complex, also moved about the country in order to celebrate the festivals of Egypt's many gods. Officials would regularly visit the palace in order to renew their attendance on the king, before returning to the various regions to exercise their delegated authority.

Titles proclaiming attendance at court

šmsw pr ꜥꜣ	follower of the palace
or *rḫ-nsw*	king's adviser

Titles associated with the ritual appearances of the king are usually compounded with the word *nsw* for 'king'.

Titles proclaiming attendance on the king

iry nfr-ḥꜣt	keeper of the royal diadem
imy-ḫnt	chamberlain (the one in front)

Titles proclaiming rank and authority delegated from the king

ḫtmty bity	king's seal-bearer
smr wꜥty	sole companion

Administrative titles are compounded with the word *bity* for 'king'. *ḫtmty-bity* is prefixed only to high-level titles. As well as signifying high rank, the title indicated that the holder was authorised to use the royal seal.

The treasury

For the monuments studied in this book, the officials attached to the treasury have particular importance:

Procurement, storage, dispensing and utilisation

m-r ḫtmt	treasurer (overseer of what is sealed)
m-r ꜥḫnwty	overseer of the chamber
ḫtmw ḫry-ꜥ	seal-bearer, assistant (to the treasurer)

The title *m-r ꜥḫnwty* was originally more general. In origin it probably referred to the 'overseer of the chamber of the residence/palace'. However, by the Middle Kingdom the title had become split between a number of different branches of the administration. A particularly common *m-r ꜥḫnwty* 'overseer of the chamber' was the *m-r ꜥḫnwty n m-r ḫtmt* 'overseer of the chamber for the treasurer', who seems to have been responsible for the procurement of raw materials (for example through mining) and for monumental building work.

Stewardship and production

	*m-r pr*	overseer of the estate (steward)
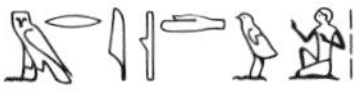	*m-r iḳdw*	overseer of builders
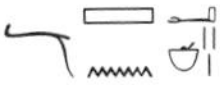	*m-r šnʿw*	overseer of the provisioning area

Regional authority

Titles associated with the government of regional districts:

	*ḥꜣty-ʿ*	governor, mayor of a town		*wḥm*	reporter, herald

Military

	*m-r mšʿ wr*	general-in-chief
	*ʿnḫ n nwt*	soldier of the town regiment

Religious titles

Titles associated with priestly functions. In the Middle Kingdom, there were few full-time priests, but élite men regularly served in the temples:

	*wʿb*	*wʿb*-priest	 or 	*it nṯr*	god's-father
	*ḥm nṯr*	*ḥm*-priest		*ḥm kꜣ*	*ka*-priest
	*ḥry sštꜣ*	master of secrets		*ẖry ḥbt*	lector priest

Although we have divided secular and religious titles for convenience here, in practice these were intertwined in élite Middle Kingdom society, where the same person could hold both secular and religious titles at once. BM EA 585, where Sarenenutet has the following titles, provides an example of this:

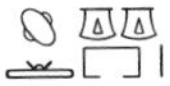	*ḥsb šnwty*	counter of the double granaries
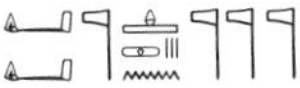	*dd ḥtp(w)-nṯr n nṯrw*	offering-giver to the gods

Titles of women

In general women were not included in the formalisation of élite society through office holding, which tended to be a male preserve (you may already have noted that most women depicted on the stelae in this book are usually referred to by their family relationship with the male owner). However, some women are shown bearing a certain range of titles which usually accord with the status of their menfolk. Of particular note for the stelae studied in this book are those of high status:

High status

 *ḥm(t)-nṯr ḥwt-ḥr* priestess of Hathor

 *ẖkrt nsw wꜥtt* sole lady in waiting

(*ẖkrt-nsw* means literally 'the king's ornament'.)

Another common title of élite women associates them with the running of the estate. It appears on stelae from the late 12th dynasty onwards:

Estate and household

 *nbt pr* lady of the house, mistress of the estate

Exercises

7.1 Signs

a. 2-consonant and 3-consonant signs

 wḏ *ḫt* *nḏm*

 *mꜣ*  *ẖr*

b. Ideograms and determinatives

SIGN		EXAMPLE		
	E58 – sail		*ṯꜣw*	breath
 or 	A10/A11 – man of rank on chair with/without flail		*šps*	dignified, august, rich
	E10 – emblem erected outside the temple of Min	 or 	*iꜣt*	office, function
	D18 – village with crossroads		*nwt*	town
	A7 – official with staff and leather grip		*sr*	official

7.2 Words

Transliterate the following words written with these signs:

 .... sweet

 .... create

 .... under, carrying

 .... command (see also §21)

 .... strong, vigorous

7.3 *A note on the writing of ỉr(ỉ) 'to do'*

A major exception to the rule on sound complements given in Chapter 2 is provided by the verb  *ỉr(ỉ)* 'to do, make' (this verb also has many idiomatic meanings). When read *ỉr,* it is generally written  alone (an exception occurs on BM EA 558 in Study Exercise 7.7 where, for space reasons, seems to be written for *ỉrr*), while  is usually to be transliterated *ỉrr* (a third form, , should always be transliterated *ỉrr*):

	*ỉr*		*ỉrr,* more rarely *ỉr*		*ỉrr*

7.4 *Translation*

Transliterate and translate the following.

a. The self-presentation section of the stela of Hekaib begins in the following way, stressing the topic of self-reliance (you may consider adding 'own' in your translation to help bring this out), compare with §49 above:

BM EA 1671, Lines 1-2:

Notes

i The hieroglyphs are organised as they are on the original, except that the elements of the passage are separated out for your convenience. You may find that you need to insert 'and' occasionally in your translation.

ii The pronoun *=f* is used to refer back to the owner of the stela as noted in §49 (as in: '**I** was an official well respected in **his** district' or the like). The switch to the third person is normal in such constructions.

iii *sẖsf* ... *r* 'to keep (something) at a distance from', idiom of impartiality.

iv *ỉwn ꜥꜣ* 'great pillar' is used metaphorically (cf. our own expression for someone being 'a tower of strength' or a 'pillar of the community')

v On the omission of the suffix pronoun *=ỉ* 'I' in writing in the third sentence, see §35 above. Read *mỉty(=ỉ) nb m nwt tn.*

b. The stela of Tjetji begins with the king's name and then Tjetji is introduced with a list of epithets:

BM EA 614, Line 1:

Notes

i is an early form of the papyrus roll . Another variant form is .

ii On the dependent pronoun *-sw,* see §41.

7.5 Stela of Ity (BM EA 586)

Transliterate and translate the following, which is the lower section of the stela given as Exercise 6.6:

BM EA 586 (lower section)

Notes

i Notice the writing of the title *it-nṯr* 'god's father' (cf. Exercise 6.6).

ii Read *mry nb=f mꜣꜥ* 'one truly beloved of his lord', where *mry* is a participle (see §50 above). *nb=f* is placed first through prestige (see §22).

VOCABULARY

	iwn	pillar		*imn-rꜥ*	(the god) Amun-Ra
	it-nṯr	god's father (priestly title)		*ity*	Ity (name)
	wꜣst	Thebes (place)		*pr*	house, estate
	mity	peer, equal		*nmtt*	journeys
	r	mouth		*ḥry-sštꜣ*	master of secrets (title)
	ḫpš	strong arm		*ḫntyt*	Khentyt (place-name)
	ḫnt(y) st	(one) foremost of position		*ḫrt-ib*	desire
	sꜣt	daughter		*sꜣt-wsrt*	Satwosret (name)

VOCABULARY (CONTINUED)

	*sꜣt-sbk*	Satsobek (name)		*swꜣ*	to pass by, surpass
	*sḫsf*	to keep at a distance		*st*	place(s)
	*šps*	dignitary (literally, 'august one')	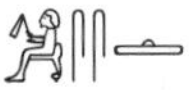	*špss*	dignity, wealth

7.6 Relative forms

The relative forms are used in a common late Middle Kingdom addition to the offering formula, which occurs on BM EA 143, the stela of Nakhti to be studied in Exercise 7.8:

The voice-offering can be extended after 'everything good and pure on which a god lives' as follows:

BM EA 143, Line 2: 

Notes

i Remember that since these are relative forms, they will require translating here with 'which'. Also consult the table in §52 for the writings.

ii See stela BM EA 143, Exercise 7.8, for vocabulary.

7.7 Study exercise: BM EA 558

The stela of Key on page 108 comes across as something of a compendium of standard expressions, rather than a smooth-running composition. Some of the sections of this inscription have already been used as examples in the main text. Transliterate and translate the stela with the help of the notes.

Notes

i For the epithets, see §§47 and 50 above.

ii For *ii m*, read *ii(.n=i) m*, parallel to *hꜣ.n=i m*. Translate *m* as 'from'.

iii For the omission of the suffix pronoun *=i*, see §35 above.

iv For *ink* + participle, see §49 above.

v *mrrt* is probably a present relative form, see §52 above.

vi For the writing of the negative ⟂ *n* as ﹏, see §38 above (in both *n ḏws(=i)* and *n wḏ(=i)*).

vii The expression *n wḏ(=i) ḥwt m s=i* is not without its difficulties. In English idiom, you may wish to translate *m* as 'for/to'.

viii There is some doubt as to whether *wḥm* should be read as a title or as part of a name *wḥm-ky*.

This inscription also introduces the important verb 'to come':

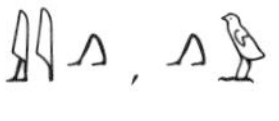 *ii* or *iw(i)* 'come' – written in two forms:
a. with monogram of 𓇋 *i* and 𓂻 walking legs
b. with walking legs ideogram

BM EA 558
(carved and painted limestone; H. 80cm)

VOCABULARY

	*wḥm*	reporter, herald (title: one who repeats)		*wḥm*	repeat
	*wḏ*	command		*mrti*	Merti (name)
	*nsw*	king		*rꜥ nb*	every day
 or 	*rḫ nsw*	king's adviser (title)		*hꜣ(i)*	descend, go down
	*ḥwt*	beating		*ḥry-tp*	chief, superior
	*ḫrp rḫ nsw*	director of king's advisers		*ḫrt-hrw*	course of the day
	*s*	man		*spꜣt*	district
	*ky*	Key (name)		*ḏws*	denounce

7.8 Study exercise: BM EA 143

Transliterate and translate the stela of Nakhti (BM EA 143) on p. 110. You may wish to make use of your work for Exercise 7.6.

VOCABULARY

	*ꜣst*	Iset, Isis (name)		*in(i)*	bring
	*pt*	sky, heavens		*mwt=f*	his mother
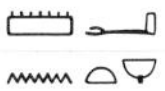	*mnꜥt*	wet-nurse		*ms-n*	born of
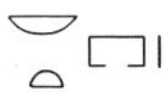	*nbt pr*	lady of the house		*nḫti*	Nakhti (name, both male and female)
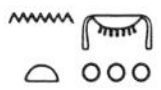	*nt-nbw*	Netnebu		*nḏm*	sweet
	*ḥꜥpy*	the inundation (as the god Hapy)		*ḥmt=f*	his wife
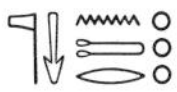	*snṯr*	incense		*kmꜣ*	create
	*st*	smell, scent		*ṯꜣw*	breath

Notes

i Translate *m* near the end of Line 2 as 'as' (an elaboration into three parts: offering, breath and incense).

ii In the writing of Abydos and Djedu the town determinative ⊗ has been expanded as though it were the word  *nwt* 'town'. However, it is still simply the determinative for Abydos and Djedu, not a separate word.

iii In the first column of women, the first sign is a writing of  *ḥm*.

iv This stela shows a number of features which place its date rather late in the sequence of stelae studied in this book. The word for Djedu is written with two *ḏd*-signs, suggesting a date of at least the late 12th dynasty. This is confirmed by the use of *n kꜣ n* without *imꜣḫ(w)* (see §26) and by the use of the *ddt pt*-formula. It is thought that the 'breath-of-life' formula only came into use in the 13th dynasty; if so, this would suggest a date in the early 13th dynasty for this stela.

BM EA 143
(carved and painted limestone; H. 81.2cm)

Chapter 8

The future

In this final chapter, we will introduce you to the 'appeal to the living' formula in which the deceased calls upon future generations to maintain his funerary cult. We will also look at the future tense used particularly to express wishes and expectations.

§53 The *sḏmty.fy* form

In expressing the future, the place of the participle is taken by the *sḏmty.fy* form: '(someone) who will/may do something'. This form has the same uses as the participles, but has its own particular endings. In its fullest writings the *sḏmty.fy* form displays the following forms:

MASCULINE	FEMININE	PLURAL (BOTH GENDERS)

sḏmty.fy	*sḏmty.sy*	*sḏmty.sn*

Often, however, the \\ *-y* of the endings is omitted:

The stela of Mentjuhotep in the Fitzwilliam Museum, Cambridge, has an appeal to the living which begins:

Fitz.E9.1922, Line 1:

ỉ ꜥnḫw tpw tꜣ ***swꜣt(y).sn*** *ḥr ỉs pn*
O the living upon the earth **who may pass** by this tomb

(See §54 below for the form of the appeal to the living and its vocabulary.)

As with participles, the *sḏmty.fy* form can be used with a noun (in this example, *swꜣt(y).sn* 'who may pass' goes with 'the living') or on its own ('someone who will do something').

§54 The appeal to the living

The *appeal to the living* formula is found on many stelae. A simple example is:

The appeal to the living of the chamberlain Minnefer (year 29 of Amenemhet II):

BM EA 829, Lines 4-5:

ỉ ʿnḫw tpw tꜣ ḥm(w)-nṯr ḥm(w)t-nṯr wʿbw nw r-pr pn
ḏd=ṯn ḫꜣ t ḥnḳt kꜣ ꜣpd n ỉmꜣḫ(w) m-r ʿḫnwty mnw-nfr mꜣʿ-ḫrw
O living ones upon the earth, the *ḥm*-priests and *ḥm*-priestesses, and the *wʿb*-priests of this temple,
may you say, 'A thousand (of) bread, beer, ox and fowl for the revered one, the overseer of the chamber Minnefer, the justified'

(See the Reference table on p. 148 for the suffix pronoun =*ṯn* 'you'.)

The appeal to the living is composed of two basic elements plus a further, optional element:

a. Hailing the visitor

The owner of the memorial addresses the passers-by; the visitors are hailed, typically in the form:

As we saw above, the stela of Mentjuhotep begins with an appeal to the living:

Fitz.E9.1922, Line 1:

ỉ ʿnḫw tpw tꜣ ...
O the living upon the earth ...

This is composed of the following words:

 or  *ỉ* O

 or  *tpw* (who are) upon

 *ʿnḫw* the living

 *tꜣ* the earth

(On the form of *tpw* 'upon', see §60 below.)

There may follow an enumeration of the people likely to pass by – such as temple staff and scribes – who are often hailed in passing the monument:

The stela of Mentjuhotep continues:

Fitz.E9.1922, Line 1:

ỉ ʿnḫw tpw tꜣ ***swꜣt(y).sn*** *ḥr ỉs pn*
O the living upon the earth **who may pass** by this tomb

As in this example, in hailing the visitor, the verb *swꜣ* 'to pass' (*ḥr* 'by') is typically used in the *sḏmty.fy* form: *swꜣty.sn* '(they) who shall pass'. *swꜣ* can be written in the following ways:

FULLER WRITINGS

 or 

ABBREVIATED WRITINGS

 or  *swꜣ* pass (by)

(Note the abbreviated writings with × D7 crossed sticks.)

b. The offering request

The owner requests that offerings or prayers be made or said for him:

From BM EA 829:

BM EA 829, Line 5:

ḏd=ṯn ḫꜣ t ḥnḳt kꜣ ꜣpd n ỉmꜣḫ(w) m-r ꜥḫnwty mnw-nfr mꜣꜥ-ḫrw
May you say, 'A thousand bread, beer, ox and fowl for the revered one, the overseer of the chamber Minnefer, the justified'

The request for saying the offering formula uses the future *sḏm(=f)* form discussed below in §55.

c. The appeal to goodwill or piety

The appeal to the living is often augmented by a third element – an invocation of the goodwill or piety of the visitors, or a declaration of the benefits visitors will gain if they make the offering. Sometimes this is included in hailing the visitors in the form of participles:

The appeal to the living of the priest Mentuhotep:

Fitz.E9.1922, Line 1:

ỉ ꜥnḫw tpw tꜣ swꜣty.sn ḥr ỉs pn
mrrw *ꜥnḫ* ***msḏḏw*** *ḫpt*
ḏd=ṯn sꜣḫ ꜣsỉr ḫnty-ỉmntw mnṯw-ḥtp
O living ones upon the earth who may pass by this tomb
and **who love** life and **who hate** death,
may you say, 'May Osiris Khentyimentu transfigure Mentjuhotep'

( *mrrw* and  *msḏḏw* are both participles; see §46 above.)

Often, however, the appeal to the goodwill or piety of the visitor takes the form of a separate clause (here beginning  *m + mrr=ṯn*) leading on to the request to say the offering:

The appeal to the living of the overseer of builders Khuenbik:

BM EA 584, Lines 3-5:

ỉ ꜥnḫw swꜣt(y).sn ḥr mꜥḥꜥt tn m ḫd m ḫsft
m mrr=ṯn šms wp-wꜣwt r nmtt=f nb
ḏd=ṯn t ḥnḳt ......

O living ones who may pass by this cenotaph in going north or in going south,
as you wish to follow Wepwawet at his journeys,
may you say, 'Bread and beer ...'

Grammatically, the first clause is sometimes introduced by *m* 'as' and the request clause sometimes by *mỉ* ('just as ..., so you should say ...')

§55 Wishes, expectations and requests: the future *sḏm(=f)*

The form used to express wishes, requests, expectations and the like is the future *sḏm(=f)*. In the appeal to the living, you have already, in fact, encountered the future *sḏm(=f)* form of *ḏd* ('say'):

The appeal to the living of the chamberlain Minnefer once more:

BM EA 829, Lines 4-5:

ỉ ꜥnḫw tpw tꜣ ḥm(w)-nṯr ḥm(w)t-nṯr wꜥbw nw r-pr -pn
ḏd=ṯn *ḫꜣ t ḥnḳt kꜣ ꜣpd n ỉmꜣḫ(w) m-r ꜥḫnwty mnw-nfr mꜣꜥ-ḫrw*
O living ones upon the earth, the *ḥm*-priests and *ḥm*-priestesses, and the *wꜥb*-priests of this temple,
may you say, 'A thousand (of) bread, beer, ox and fowl for the revered one, the overseer of the chamber Minnefer, the justified'

The future *sḏm(=f)* is a form distinct from the present *sḏm(=f)* noted in §42 above (although the two can be difficult to distinguish by the writings alone). The future *sḏm(=f)*, for example, is not used with auxiliaries such as *ỉw*. Its full forms are given in §59 below (you may wish to compare the writings of the two forms in the reference tables on pp. 145 and 146).

§56 The Abydos formula

The Abydos formula is a fairly standardised set of afterlife wishes. The mature version belongs to the first half of the 12th dynasty with earlier (less standardised) versions occurring in the 11th dynasty. The full formula has twenty elements (as in BM EA 567), but many texts contain a selection:

A brief version of the Abydos formula occurs on BM EA 162:

BM EA 162, Lines 4-6:

dỉ.t(w) *n=f ꜥwy m nšmt ḥr wꜣ(w)t ỉmnt*
šsp=f *ḥtpt ḥr ḥtp ꜥꜣ m ḥb(w) n ẖrt-nṯr*
ḏd.t(w) *n=f ỉw m ḥtp ỉn wr(w) n ꜣbḏw m wꜣg m ḏḥwtt ...*

> **May** hands/help **be given** to him in the Neshmet-bark on the ways of the west;
> **May he receive** offerings on the great altar on the festivals of the necropolis;
> **May** 'Welcome in peace' **be said** for him by the great of Abydos: on the Wag-festival and on the Thoth-festival ... (a list of festivals follows)

(*.t(w)* is the affix of the passive with *ỉn* used for 'by' ('may something be done by someone').

You will be studying this formula in the Exercises to this chapter.

§57 Purpose and causation

a. Purpose/result clauses

The future *sḏm(=f)* is also used to express purpose or result ('so that', 'in order that'). This is the form used in the offering formula:

The offering formula from BM EA 558:

BM EA 558, Lines 1-2:

ḥtp-dỉ-nsw ꜣsỉr nb ḏdw nṯr ꜥꜣ nb ꜣbḏw
***dỉ=f** prt-ḫrw t ḥnḳt kꜣ ꜣpd šs mnḫt ...*
An offering which the king gives to Osiris lord of Djedu, great god, lord of Abydos,
so that he might give an invocation offering of bread, beer, ox and fowl, alabaster and linen ...

b. Causation

We have already noted the use of the verb *rdỉ* to express causation when followed by another verb with the sense of 'to cause/have/let/allow someone to do something' (see §40). This other verb goes in the future *sḏm(=f)* form:

Ikhernofret's description of the great procession of Osiris:

Berlin 1204, Lines 18-19:

*ỉw ỉr.n=ỉ prt ꜥꜣt šms=ỉ nṯr r nmtt=f dỉ.n=ỉ **sḳd** dpt-nṯr*
I conducted the great procession, following the god at his travels, and I made the god's boat **sail**

§58 Negation

The future *sḏm(=f)* in its main usage is negated by ***nn* + *future sḏm(=f)***: 'you will/may not do that':

The bottom section of BM EA 101 is based on the goodwill and wish elements of the appeal to the living (i.e. that good things will happen to passers-by when they say the offering formula for the deceased):

BM EA 101, Lines 2-4: 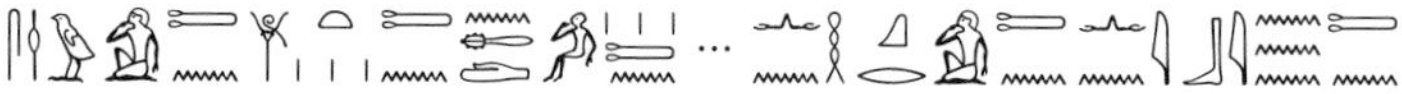

swḏ=ṯn ỉꜣ(w)t=ṯn n ẖrd(w)=ṯn ... nn ḥḳr=ṯn nn ỉbỉ=ṯn
You will hand over your offices to your children ... you will not be hungry, you will not be thirsty

§59 Forms of the *sḏmty.fy* and the future *sḏm(=f)*

The *sḏmty.fy* and the future *sḏm(=f)* have the following forms:

a. sḏmty.fy

	SINGULAR		PLURAL
	MASCULINE	FEMININE	
STRONG	 *sḏmty.fy*	 *sḏmty.sy*	 *sḏmty.sn*
DOUBLING - doubling	 *mꜣꜣty.fy*	 *mꜣꜣty.sy*	 *mꜣꜣty.sn*
WEAK	 *šdty.fy*	 *šdty.sy*	 *šdty.sn*
EXTRA WEAK - *rdỉ* shows *r*	 *rdỉty.fy*	 *rdỉty.sy*	 *rdỉty.sn*
ỉy(ỉ)/ỉw(ỉ) - shows *ỉw*	 *ỉwty.fy*	 *ỉwty.sy*	 *ỉwty.sn*

b. The future sḏm(=f):

	FUTURE *sḏm(=f)*		
STRONG		*sḏm=f*	may he hear
DOUBLING - no doubling		*mꜣ=f*	may he see
WEAK	 or 	*mr=f* or *mry=f*	may he love
EXTRA WEAK		*dỉ=f* (no *r*)	may he give
SPECIAL CASES		*ỉwt=f* (with extra *-t*)	may he come
		*ỉnt=f* (with extra *-t*)	may he bring

Notes

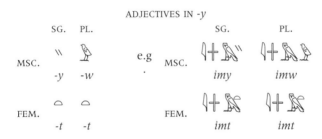

i The verb *mꜣꜣ* 'to see' also displays a form *mꜣn=f*.
ii The weak verb form with *-y* is most common in the first person.
iii The forms from the verbs 'come' and 'bring' show an extra *t*.

§60 Adjectives in *-y*

When used with nouns, a special adjective form of the preposition is used:

The stela of Mentjuhotep:

Fitz.E9.1922, Line 1: *ỉ ꜥnḫw* ***tpw*** *tꜣ* ...
O the living **(who are) upon** the earth ...

Here *tpw* is an adjective derived from the preposition *tp* ('upon'). As an adjective *tpw* agrees with the noun *ꜥnḫw* (both show the plural *-w*). This form is termed the *adjective in -y* (the *-y* only occurs in the masculine singular form). Some prepositions display a distinctive writing in the adjective in *-y*:

PREPOSITION		ADJECTIVE IN *-y*	
m	in	*ỉmy*	(which/who is) in
r	at, towards in relation to	*ỉry*	(which/who is) at, towards, relating to
ḥr	upon	*ḥry*	(which/who is) upon
ḫnt	in front	*ḫnty*	(which/who is) in front
ẖr	under, carrying	*ẖry*	(which/who is) under, carrying
tp	upon	or *tpy*	(which/who is) upon

Adjectives in *-y* agree with their nouns in number and gender:

ADJECTIVES IN *-y*

	SG.	PL.			SG.	PL.
MSC.	*-y*	*-w*	e.g.	MSC.	*ỉmy*	*ỉmw*
FEM.	*-t*	*-t*		FEM.	*ỉmt*	*ỉmt*

In writing, however, *-y* and *-w* are often omitted:

The stela of Inhuretnakht begins with an offering formula invoking Anubis:

BM EA 1783, Line 1:
ḥtp-di-nsw inpw ***tp(y)*** *ḏw=f* ***im(y)*** *wt nb tꜣ ḏsr*
An offering which the king gives (to) Anubis who is **upon** his mountain, **the one in** the *wt*-fetish, lord of the sacred land

Adjectives in *-y* are common in titles, for example:

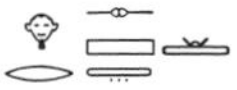	*ḥry-sštꜣ*	master of secrets (literally, the one upon secrets)		*ḥry-ḥbt*	lector priest (literally, the one carrying the lector book)

Like other adjectives, the adjectives in *-y* can be used on their own ('the one who ...', 'the thing which ...'). A particular example is the name of Khentyimentu 'the foremost of the westerners':

The stela of Khuenbik begins with an offering formula invoking Osiris:

BM EA 584, Line 1:
ḥtp-di-nsw ꜣsir nb ḏdw ***ḫnty-imntw*** *(nṯr) ꜥꜣ nb ꜣbḏw*
An offering which the king gives to Osiris lord of Djedu, **Khentyimentu**, great (god), lord of Abydos

(*nṯr* has been omitted in the phrase *nṯr ꜥꜣ* 'great god')

imntw is also an adjective in *-y*, derived from the noun *imnt* 'the west' and means 'the ones of the west','westerners'. So *ḫnty-imntw* means 'the one at the front of the westerners' (the 'westerners' are the dead, the people in the realm of sunset).

VOCABULARY

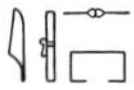	*is*	tomb		*mnw-nfr*	Minnefer
	*mnṯw-ḥtp*	Mentjuhotep		*msḏ(i)*	hate
	*r-pr*	temple		*ḥm(w)-nṯr*	*ḥm*-priests
	*ḥm(w)t-nṯr*	*ḥm*-priestesses		*ḫpt*	death
	*sꜣḫ*	transfigure			

Exercises

8.1 Signs

a. 2-consonant and 3-consonant signs:

	ꜣḫ		*šn*		*šsp*
	is		*tp*		*ꜥḥꜥ*

b. Three other signs which are useful at this point:

SIGN		EXAMPLE		
or	E30/E31 – combination of E29 and D32 (and C11 – sandy hill-slope)	or	*ẖrt-nṯr*	necropolis, cemetery
	E17 – dagger. Used in the adjective in *-y tpy*		*tpy*	(who is) upon. See §60 above
	E33 – two planks crossed and joined. Used in the adjective in *-y imy*.		*imy*	(who is) in. See §60 above

8.2 Words

Transliterate the following words:

	....	receive, take		....	transfigure
	....	tomb, cenotaph		....	entourage
	....	tomb		....	akh-spirit

(The blessed dead become *ꜣḫ*-spirits in the afterlife by being transfigured (*sꜣḫ*) after death.)

8.3 BM EA 567

BM EA 567 (shown on p. 120) begins with a date, an offering formula, and then moves onto a full set of the twenty elements of the Abydos formula, of which a selection are given here, including some mentioning the Abydos mysteries. Ignore the sections in grey.

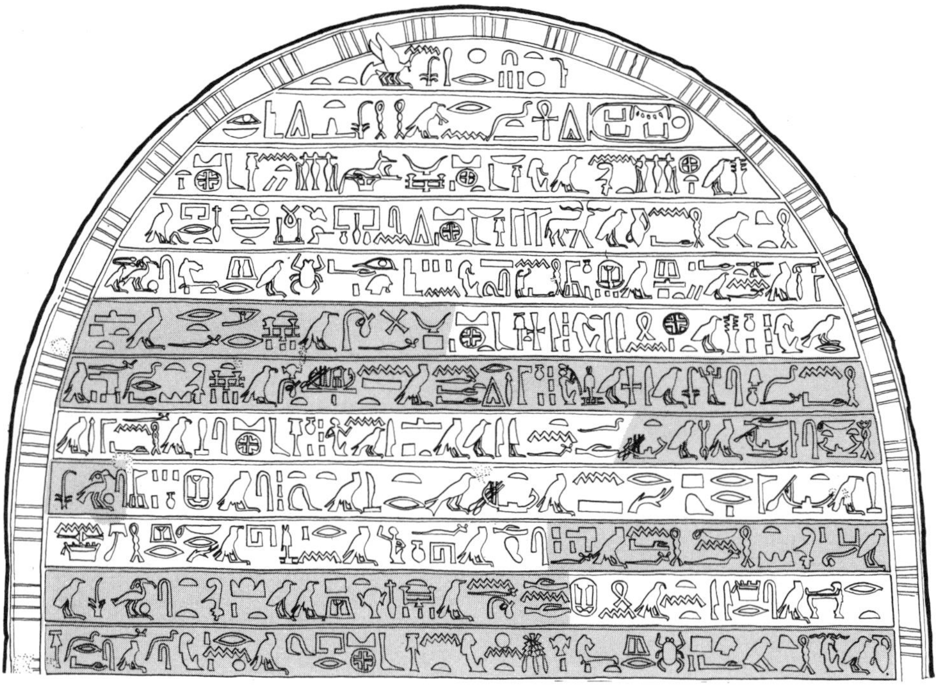

BM EA 567
(carved limestone; w. 63.5cm)

Notes

i See notes to Exercise 7.8 for the writing of the determinative of *ḏdw* and *ꜣbḏw*.

ii Wepwawet has the epithet *ḫnty ꜣbḏw* 'the one at the front/head of Abydos' (see §60 above for *ḫnty*).

iii The names of Heket and Khnum are written with their frog and ram determinatives respectively.

iv *ḫt -nbt nfr(t) pr(r)t m-bꜣḥ nṯr ꜥꜣ* 'everything good which goes before the great god'. *pr(r)t* is a participle.

v In Line 5 the Abydos formula begins with *ms.t(w) -n=f ꜥwy ḫr* ... 'May arms be presented to him carrying ...' The two groups of the venerated dead noted are *šms(w) n ꜣsir* 'the followers of Osiris' and *tp(w)-ꜥ ḫprw ḫr-ḥꜣt* 'the ancestors who existed before'.

vi In Line 5 *-ṯw* is the dependent pronoun 'you' (the owner Amenemhet is sometimes referred to as 'he' sometimes as 'you'). See §41.

vii On *šnyt imt ꜣbḏw*, see §60.

viii In Line 8 *ḏ* in *ḏd* is flatter than the normal form. Notice that it does not have the horns of the *f*-viper.

ix Translate *nšmt wrt r nmtt=s* as 'when the great *nšmt*-bark is at its journeys'.

x In Line 10 *tꜣ-wr*, the nome containing Abydos, here refers to the inhabitant of the nome, hence it can have a 'mouth'.

xi Insert 'at' in your translation before *ḥꜣkr* in Line 10.

xii The vigil of Horus-*šn* or Horus the fighter remains one of the most elusive aspects of the Osiris mysteries, although it probably refers to part of the rites concerned with the reanimation of the dead Osiris.

When you have finished both Exercises 8.3 and 8.5, you may wish to compare the Abydos formulae on the two stelae.

VOCABULARY

ỉỉw	welcome	*ꜥwy*	arms
wr(w)	the great	*m-bꜣḥ*	before
ms	present, offer	*r-pḳr*	Ro-Poker (Poker)
ḥꜣkr	Haker-rites	*ḥnw*	jubilation
ḥnꜥ	together with	*ḥtp*	offerings, peace
ḫnty	(the one) at the front	*ẖr*	carrying, under
sdm < *sḏm*	hear (the *ḏ* has changed into *d* over time)	*sḏꜣ*	travel
sḏrt	vigil	*šmsw*	followers
šnyt	entourage	*grḥ*	night
tꜣ-wr	Tawer (nome)	*tp(w)-ꜥ*	ancestors

sḏryt nt ḥr-šn	the vigil of Horus-*šn*

8.4 Study exercise: BM EA 584

Transliterate and translate the stela of Khuenbik (BM EA 584 shown on p. 122) with its appeal to the living.

Note

In Lines 4–5 *m mrr=ṯn šms wp-wꜣwt r nmtt=f nb* 'as you wish to follow Wepwawet at all his journeys'; *šms* is in the infinitive form and supplies the object of the wish.

BM EA 584
(carved limestone; H. 53cm)

VOCABULARY

	m ḫsft	in going south		*m ḫd*	in going north
or	*m-r iḳdw*	overseer of builders		*mʿḥʿt*	cenotaph, tomb
	mꜣi-n-ḥr	Maienhor (name)		*ptḥ-ḥtp*	Ptahhotep (name)
	n-ptḥ-kꜣw	Niptahkau (name)		*nmtt*	journeys

VOCABULARY (CONTINUED)

	rn	name		*rrwt*	Rerut (name)
	ḥḳt	(the goddess) Heket		*ḥtp*	offerings
	ḫw-n-bik	Khuenbik (name)		*ẖnmw*	(the god) Khnum
	sʿnḫ	make live, perpetuate		*smyt imntt*	the western desert
	šms	to follow		*ḏf(ꜣw)*	provisions

8.5 Study exercise: BM EA 162

The final stela for you to study is BM EA 162, the stela of the general-in-chief Ameny. The stela is shown on p. 125. As usual, transliterate and translate with the help of the accompanying vocabulary.

Notes

i See Exercise 3.6 for vocabulary for the offering formula section.

ii See Chapter 7 for the structure of the various epithets.

VOCABULARY

or	*iw* or *iiw*	welcome	or	*ʿwy*	arms
or	*wr(w)*	the great		*ḥb(w)*	festivals
	ḥtp	peace, satisfaction		*ḥtpt*	offerings
	ḥtp ʿꜣ	great altar		*šsp*	receive

FESTIVALS

	wꜣg	Wag-festival		*prt mnw*	procession of Min
	ḏḥwtt	Thoth-festival		*prt spdt*	procession of Sothis
	ḥb skr	Soker-festival		*tp-rnpt*	beginning of the lunar year

TITLES AND OCCUPATIONS

	ḥm-nṯr ḥwt-ḥr	priestess of Hathor		*m-r ḫtmt*	treasurer
	ḥm-kꜣ	ka-priest		*m-r mšʿ wr*	general-in-chief
	wbꜣt	cup-bearer		*nšt*	hairdresser

TITLES AND OCCUPATIONS (CONTINUED)

	*ḥry-pr*	domestic servant

NAMES

	*imny*	Ameny
	*ḫwyt*	Khuyet
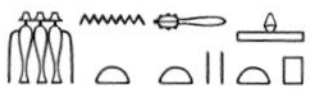	*ḫnt-ḫty-ḥtp*	Khenetkhetyhetep
	*sꜣ-ḥwt-ḥr*	Sahathor
	*sꜣt-sbk*	Satsobek
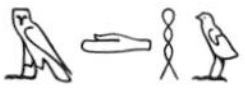	*mdḥw*	Medhu
	*sꜣ-ḫnt-ḫty*	Sakhenetkhety
	*sꜣwtyt*	Sautyt
	*sꜣt-ḫnt-ḫti*	Satkhenetkhety
	*ḳbw*	Kebu
	*ḏfꜣ-ḥꜥp(y)*	Djefahapy

Once you have read this stela, it will no doubt strike you that the owner himself is actually missing from the figures shown. This is because, like a number of stelae from Abydos, BM EA 162 belongs to a group dedicated in an offering-chapel at the site. Unfortunately, Abydos was cleared of many of its Middle Kingdom monuments by collectors and early archaeologists in the nineteenth century without a proper record being made of the find-sites. It is only through the work of scholars scouring the museum collections of the world and sifting through the sparse archaeological record that original groups of stelae are gradually being reassembled.

Fortunately, BM EA 162 has been allocated to a group now known conventionally as Abydos North Offering Chapel (ANOC) 2. It has a companion, now in the Egyptian Museum, Cairo (CCG 20546), which shows the same style and phraseology: the two were clearly made in the same workshop as a pair. It too lacks a figure of Ameny himself; instead it depicts further relatives and dependants looking from left to right (whereas in BM EA 162 they look from right to left). This pair of stelae no doubt framed a central stela depicting Ameny himself; one piece which has been proposed is in the Musée du Louvre, Paris (C35).

BM EA 162
(carved limestone; H. 113cm)

About the Front Cover

The cover shows a detail of an inscribed ritual tool used in the rite of 'opening the mouth' – an obscure ceremony designed to breathe life into an embalmed corpse, a statue or an inscribed image. The text records a dedication from Senwosret I to his celebrated predecessor (here termed *ỉt* '(fore)father'), Mentjuhotep II of the 11th Dynasty, who is here identified by his praenomen Nebhepetre.

MMA 24.21: *nṯr nfr nb tꜣwy s-n-wsrt*
ỉr.n=f m mnw=f n ỉt=f nb-ḥpt-rꜥ mꜣꜥ-ḫrw

The perfect god, the lord of the twin lands, Senwosret:
he has made his dedication for his father,
Nebhepetre, the justified.

mnw 'dedication' refers here to the opening of the mouth implement itself and the rites associated with it. *mnw* is often translated as 'monument' in dictionaries, but actually refers more generally to royal dedications, here for a celebrated royal predecessor.

The appearance of an extra *m* before the object *mnw* is a standard part of this dedication formula, although the reason for it is still disputed by scholars (as indeed are the intricacies of the grammar of the formula) – so you certainly should not worry too much about it. According to one suggestion, it indicates that it is the dedication of the object itself which is seen as the focal-point of the formula, focusing on Senwosret's performance of the commemorative functions of kingship through supplying the opening of the mouth implement for the animation of statues of his celebrated predecessor.

VOCABULARY

	*mnw*	dedication		*nb-ḥpt-rꜥ*	Nebhepetre

Hieroglyphic sign-lists for the exercises

The following lists are intended to help you to identify particular hieroglyphs quickly and easily, and then work out how they have been used to write words. You can also, if you wish, treat them as a convenient resource for memorising some of the most commonly used hieroglyphs.

List I: 1-consonant signs

ꜣ	𓄿	Called *aleph*. Originally a throaty trill, it later became a stop, as in cockney pronunciation of *bottle* as *bo'l*, and *a hat* as *a 'a'*
i͗	𓇋	Called *yodh*. Originally a stop, it tended to sound more like *y*. A weak sound, often not written
y	1 𓇌 2 𓏭	Like *y* in *yes*
ꜥ	𓂝	Called *ayin*. A throaty gurgle, like saying *a* whilst swallowing
w	1 𓅱 2 𓏲	Called *waw*. Like *w* in *wet*. A weak sound, often not written
b	𓃀	Like *b* in *bet*
p	𓊪	Like *p* in *pet*
f	𓆑	Like *f* in *fit*
m	𓅓	Like *m* in *met*
n	𓈖	Like *n* in *net*
r	𓂋	Like *r* in *rain*, but distinctly trilled as in Scots pronunciation
h	𓉔	Like *h* in *home*
ḥ	𓎛	Emphatic *h* pronounced in the throat
ḫ	𓐍	Like Scots *ch* in *loch*
ẖ	𓄡	Slightly softer than *ḫ*, like German *ch* in *ich*
s	1 𓋴 2 𓊃	Like *s* in *soap*
š	𓈙	Like *sh* in *ship*
ḳ	𓈎	*k* pronounced at back of mouth, like Arabic *q* in *Qurʿân* (Koran)
k	𓎡	Like *k* in *kit*
g	𓎼	Like *g* in *get*
t	𓏏	Like *t* in *tub*
ṯ	𓍿	Like *t* in British pronunciation of *tune*
d	𓂧	Like *d* in *did*
ḏ	𓆓	Like *j* in *joke*, or French *di* in *dieu*

List II: Some common 2-consonant signs

ꜣw	*bꜣ*	*nb*	*ḫt*	*ḳd*
ꜣb or *mr*	*bḥ* or *ḥw*	*nm*	*ẖꜣ*	*kꜣ*
ꜣḫ	*pꜣ*	*nn*	*ẖn*	*km*
ỉw	*pr*	*nḥ*	*ẖn*	*gm*
ỉn or *nw*	*pḥ*	*ns*	*ẖr*	*gs*
ỉr	*mꜣ*	*nḏ*	*sꜣ*	*tꜣ*
ỉs	*mỉ*	*ḥꜣ*	*sꜣ*	*tỉ*
or *ꜥꜣ*	*mw*	*ḥw* or *bḥ*	*sꜣ*	*tp*
ꜥḳ	*mn*	*ḥm*	*sw*	*tm*
ꜥḏ	*mr*	*ḥn*	*sn*	*ṯꜣ*
wꜣ	*mr*	*ḥr*	*sk* or *wꜣḥ*	*ḏꜣ*
wꜥ	*mr* or *ꜣb*	*ḥs*	*šꜣ*	*ḏw*
wp	*mḥ*	*ḥḏ*	*šw*	*ḏr*
wn	*ms*	*ḫꜣ*	*šn*	*ḏd*
wr	*mt*	*ḫꜥ*	*šs*	
wḏ	*m(w)t*	*ḫw*	*šd*	

List III: Some common 3-consonant signs

ỉꜣm or *ỉmꜣ*	*wꜣḥ* or *sk*	*mꜣꜥ*	*ḥꜣt*	*ḫnt*	*sšm*
ỉwn	*wꜥb*	*nbw*	*ḥḳꜣ*	*ḫrw*	*šps*
ꜥnḫ	*wḥm*	*nfr*	*ḥtp*	*ẖnm*	*šms*
ꜥḥꜥ	*wsr*	*nṯr*	*ḫpr*	*spd*	*dwꜣ*

List IV: Some common ideograms

=ỉ	I, my (§36)	*ỉwn*	pillar	*ꜥḥ*	palace
ỉꜣt	office	*ỉb*	heart	*ꜥḥꜣ*	fight
ỉꜣw	praise	*ỉmnt*	west	*wꜣt*	road, way
ỉỉ	come	*ꜥ*	arm	*wꜥb*	pure

	*pr*	house, estate		*rnpt*	year		*sr*	official
	*mšʿ*	expedition		*rd(i)*	give		*sḫt*	countryside
	n	not (§39)		*rdwy*	legs		*sḏm*	hear
	*nwt*	town		*ḥ3t*	front		*špsy*	dignified
	*nmtt*	step, journey		*ḥr*	(1) face (2) on		*k3*	ox, bull
	*nṯr*	god		*ḥtp*	offering	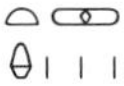	*t*	bread
	*nḏm*	sweet		*st*	seat, place		*t3*	land
	*r*	mouth		*sp3t*	district		*tp*	upon
	*rʿ*	sun		*smsw*	elder, eldest		*ḏsr*	(1) clear (2) sacred

List V: Full Sign List

What follows is a complete list of signs appearing in this book, with an explanation of the different ways in which each one has been used to write words. Since this is a practical list designed to help you find an unfamiliar sign quickly, more recognisable signs have been grouped into three broad categories (humans, animals, nature), whilst others have been grouped by shape (small, tall, broad). The signs are given here in a standardised font, but it should be remembered that there will be some variation in their forms as they appear on monuments; in particular, the details of a sign will be affected by whether it is painted (as on a coffin) or inscribed (as on a stela).

Readers who continue their study of ancient Egyptian will eventually need to become familiar with the systematic sign-list of Gardiner's *Egyptian Grammar* (see p. 176). Since Gardiner used many more categories than we have, there is no correspondence between his list and ours in the way a particular sign is classified. Here, we have used the following abbreviations: 1c., one-consonant sign; 2c., two-consonant sign; 3c., three-consonant sign; abb., abbreviation; det., determinative; ideo., ideogram; com., sign combined with other elements.

Index

§A. Signs depicting people or parts of the human body

A1 A2 A3 A4 A5 A6 A7 A8 A9 A10 A11 A12

A13 A14 A15 A16 A17 A18 A19 A20 A21 A22 A23 A24
A25 A26 A27 A28 A29 A30 A31 A32 A33 A34 A35 A36
A37 A38 A39 A40 A41 A42 A43 A44 A45 A46 A47 A48
A49 A50 A51 A52 A53 A54 A55 A56 A57 A58 A59 A60
A61 A62

§B. Signs depicting creatures or parts of their bodies

B1 B2 B3 B4 B5 B6 B7 B8 B9 B10 B11 B12
B13 B14 B15 B16 B17 B18 B19 B20 B21 B22 B23 B24
B25 B26 B27 B28 B29 B30 B31 B32 B33 B34 B35 B36
B37 B38 B39 B40 B41 B42 B43 B44 B45 B46 B47 B48
B49 B50 B51 B52 B53 B54 B55 B56 B57 B58 B59 B60
B61 B62 B63 B64 B65 B66 B67

§C. Signs involving sky, earth, water, or plants

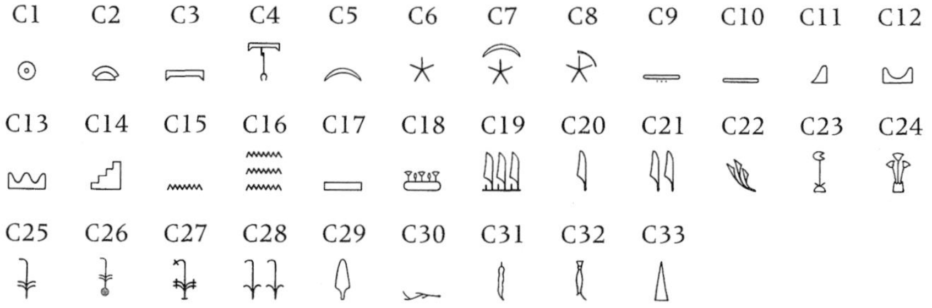
C1 C2 C3 C4 C5 C6 C7 C8 C9 C10 C11 C12
C13 C14 C15 C16 C17 C18 C19 C20 C21 C22 C23 C24
C25 C26 C27 C28 C29 C30 C31 C32 C33

§D. Other small signs

D1 D2 D3 D4 D5 D6 D7 D8 D9 D10 D11 D12
D13 D14 D15 D16 D17 D18 D19 D20 D21 D22 D23 D24
D25 D26 D27 D28 D29 D30 D31 D32 D33 D34 D35 D36
D37 B45

§E. Other tall signs

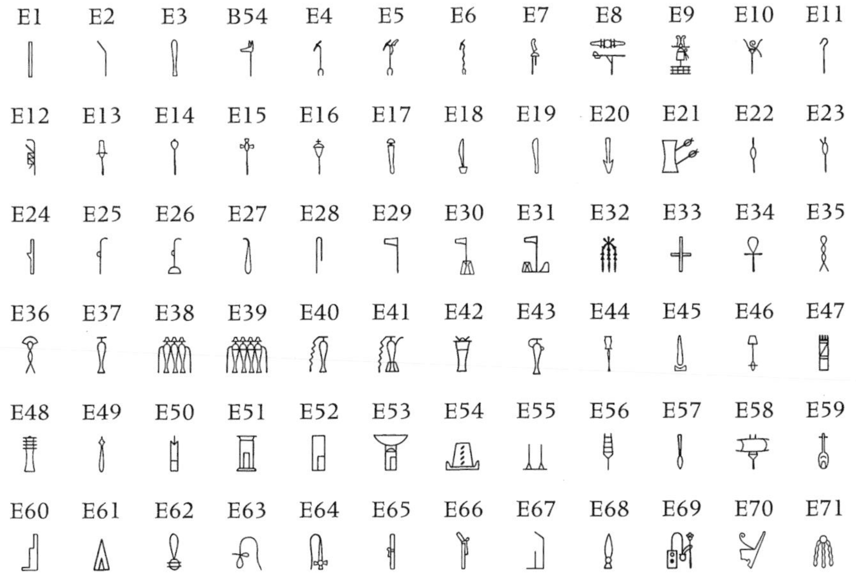
E1 E2 E3 B54 E4 E5 E6 E7 E8 E9 E10 E11
E12 E13 E14 E15 E16 E17 E18 E19 E20 E21 E22 E23
E24 E25 E26 E27 E28 E29 E30 E31 E32 E33 E34 E35
E36 E37 E38 E39 E40 E41 E42 E43 E44 E45 E46 E47
E48 E49 E50 E51 E52 E53 E54 E55 E56 E57 E58 E59
E60 E61 E62 E63 E64 E65 E66 E67 E68 E69 E70 E71

§F. Other broad signs

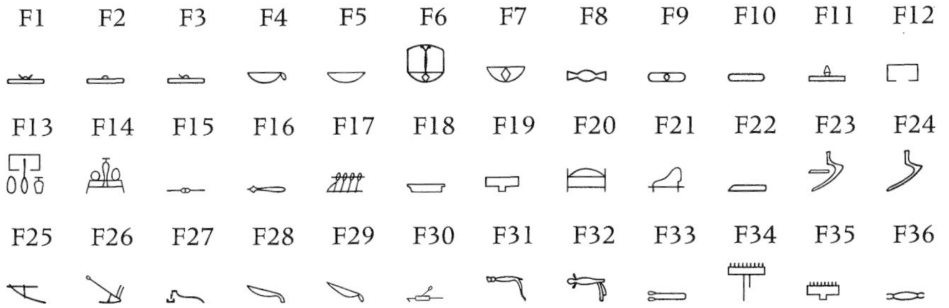
F1 F2 F3 F4 F5 F6 F7 F8 F9 F10 F11 F12
F13 F14 F15 F16 F17 F18 F19 F20 F21 F22 F23 F24
F25 F26 F27 F28 F29 F30 F31 F32 F33 F34 F35 F36

F37 F38 F39 F40 F41 F42 F43 F44 F45 F46 F47 F48

F49 F50 F51 F52 F53 F54 F55 F56 F57

Full list

§A. Signs depicting people or parts of the human body

A1		man seated	(1) det. man, occupations of men; (2) ideo. or det. 'I, me, my' (§36, §41, §49)
A2		woman seated	det. woman, occupations of women
A3		god seated	det. god, names/titles of gods
A4		goddess with feather on head	ideo. or det. *mꜣꜥt* 'harmony', especially if personified as a goddess (compare with B27)
A5		man seated with hand to mouth	det. eat, speak, emotion (§6)
A6		man kneeling in adoration	det. *hnw* 'jubilation'
A7		official with staff and leather grip	(1) ideo. *sr* 'official'; (2) hence det. official
A8		man leaning on forked stick	ideo. *smsw* 'elder, eldest'
A9		old man leaning on stick	det. or abb. *iꜣw* 'old'
A10		official holding flail	(1) ideo. *špsy* 'dignified' and related words; (2) det. deceased official
A11		official seated	alternative form of A10
A12		man striking two-handed with staff	det. effort, action, violence
A13		man striking	ideo. or det. *ḥwi* 'strike'
A14		man building wall	(1) det. build; (2) abb. *iḳd* 'builder'
A15		man falling	det. fall, fell, overthrow
A16		man falling with blood streaming	det. enemy
A17		man gesturing	det. *i* the interjection 'O!'
A18		man standing with hand to mouth	det. *srḫ* 'talk about, accuse'
A19		man with arms raised in joy	det. rejoice
A20		man with arms in adoration	(1) abb. *dwꜣ* 'adore'; (2) hence det. adore
A21		man slumped	det. tired, weak

A22	woman giving birth	det. give birth
A23	infant	(1) det. child; (2) hence abb. *ẖrd* 'child'; (3) 2c. *nn* (or *nnỉ*)
A24	soldier	ideo. or det. *mšꜥ* 'expedition, army'
A25	man seated with dagger	ideo. or det. *ỉry* 'keeper'
A26	royal figure with flail	(1) variant of A27; (2) det. *ḫnty-ỉmntw* (a name of the god Osiris)
A27	royal figure	(1) abb. *nsw* 'king'; (2) det. names of the god Osiris
A28	figure of Amun	ideo. *ỉmn* '(the god) Amun'
A29	priest com. water pouring from jug	(1) alternative for A55; (2) hence ideo. *wꜥb* 'priest'
A30	mummy on bier	det. lying down, death
A31	face	(1) ideo. *ḥr* 'face', 'on'; (2) hence 2c. *ḥr*
A32	head in profile	(1) ideo. *tp* 'head', 'upon'; (2) hence 2c. *tp*
A33	hair	det. hair
A34	front of face	det. face, nose, e.g. *sn* 'kiss'
A35	eyes com. falcon markings	ideo. *ptr* 'observe, view'
A36	eye	(1) 2c. *ỉr*; (2) det. *mꜣꜣ* 'see'
A37	eye with cosmetic	det. actions or conditions of the eye
A38	mouth	(1) ideo. *r* 'mouth'; (2) hence 1c. *r*
A39	hand	1c. *d*
A40	arm	(1) ideo. *ꜥ* 'arm'; (2) hence 1c. *ꜥ*; (3) often alternative for A41–44
A41	arm offering loaf (E61)	(1) ideo. *dỉ* or *rdỉ* 'give', alternative for E61; (2) read *m* or *mỉ* in the names *bꜣ-mkt* and *dwꜣ-mwt=f* by confusion with another sign
A42	arm holding stick	det. action, violence, effort, alternative for A12
A43	arm holding flail	2c. *ḫw*
A44	arm holding wand or lettuce	ideo. *ḏsr* 'sacred' and related words
A45	arms holding shield and axe	ideo. *ꜥḥꜣ* 'fight' and related words
A46	arms rowing	2c. *ḫn*
A47	arms gesturing denial	ideo. the negative words *n* (§39) and *nn* (§58)
A48	arms raised	(1) ideo. *kꜣ* 'ka'; (2) hence 2c. *kꜣ*
A49	arms com. E3	abb. *ḥm-kꜣ* 'ka-priest'

A50		boat's mast (E56) com. A40	3c. *ꜥḥꜥ*, alternative for E56
A51		breast	det. breast, suckle
A52		penis	(1) det. male; (2) 2c. *mt*
A53		penis with issue of fluid	det. or abb. *bꜣḥ* in *m-bꜣḥ* 'in the presence of'
A54		lower leg	1c. *b*
A55		A54 com. water pouring from jug	ideo. or det. *wꜥb* 'pure' and related words
A56		leg	(1) ideo. or det. *rd* 'leg'; (2) det. tread
A57		legs walking	(1) det. motion; (2) ideo. *ỉw(ỉ)* 'come'; (3) ideo. *nmtt* '(formal) journey'
A58		C20 com. A57	combined sound-sign and det. for *ỉỉ* 'come'
A59		D33 com. A57	combined sound-sign and det. for *ỉn(ỉ)* 'bring'
A60		F15 com. A57	combined sound-sign and det. for words suggesting motion which include the sound *s*, e.g. *sb(ỉ)* 'go', *ms* 'bring'
A61		F29 com. A57	combined sound-sign and det. for *sšm* 'conduct' and related words, alternative for F29
A62		F33 com. A57	combined sound-sign and det. for *ỉṯ(ỉ)* 'seize'

§B. Signs depicting creatures or parts of their bodies.

B1		quail chick	1c. *w*
B2		owl	1c. *m*
B3		Egyptian vulture	1c. *ꜣ*
B4		pair of vultures	variant of B3 when writing *ꜣꜣ*
B5		buzzard	2c. *tw*, especially at the end of words, often confused with B3
B6		guinea-fowl	2c. *nḥ*
B7		pintail duck	(1) 2c. *sꜣ*; (2) det. bird, alternative for B8
B8		white-fronted goose	(1) 2c. *gb*; (2) det. bird
B9		duck in flight	2c. *pꜣ*
B10		trussed goose or duck	det. goose
B11		head of duck	abb. *ꜣpd* 'bird'
B12		duckling	2c. *ṯꜣ*
B13		pair of plovers	ideo. or det. *rḫty* 'washerman'

B14		cormorant	2c. *ꜥḳ*
B15		jabiru	2c. *bꜣ*
B16		human-headed bird com. bowl	ideo. *bꜣ* 'soul' (New Kingdom)
B17		falcon	(1) det. falcon; (2) hence ideo. *ḥr* '(the god) Horus'
B18		B17 com. E52	ideo. *ḥwt-ḥr* '(the goddess) Hathor'
B19		falcon perched	det. gods
B20		falcon-headed god	ideo. *rꜥ* '(the god) Re'
B21		sparrow	det. small, weak, pathetic
B22		swallow	2c. *wr*
B23		vulture	(1) ideo. *mwt* 'mother'; (2) hence 2c. *mt*
B24		black ibis	(1) ideo. *gm* 'find'; (2) hence 2c. *gm*
B25		crested ibis	2c. *ꜣḫ* in *ꜣḫ* '*akh*-spirit' and related words
B26		sacred ibis	ideo. *ḏḥwty* '(the god) Thoth'
B27		feather	(1) 2c. *šw*; (2) abb. *mꜣꜥt* 'harmony'
B28		egg	ideo. or det. *ꜣst* '(the goddess) Isis'
B29		ox	ideo. or det. ox, bull, cattle
B30		head of ox	abb. *kꜣ* 'ox'
B31		calf	det. cattle
B32		new-born calf	2c. *ỉw*
B33		kid	2c. *ỉb*
B34		ram	det. ram, sheep
B35		B34 com. bowl	abb. *bꜣ* 'ram'
B36		hide of goat	2c. *ẖn*
B37		hide pierced by arrow	det. pierce
B38		piece of flesh	(1) det. flesh; (2) ideo. *ꜣst* '(the goddess) Isis'
B39		foreleg of ox	ideo. or det. *ḫpš* 'foreleg' (of animal), 'strong arm' (of man)
B40		leg of ox	3c. *wḥm*
B41		animal belly with tail	1c. *ẖ*
B42		ox horns	2c. *wp*
B43		ox ear	ideo. or det. *sḏm* 'hear'

B44		ox tongue	(1) ideo. *m-r* 'overseer' (§24b); (2) 2c. *ns*
B45		heart	ideo. or det. *ỉb* 'heart'
B46		spine with issue of marrow	det. or abb. *ỉmꜣḫ* 'veneration' and related words
B47		spine with issue of marrow at ends	2c. *ꜣw*
B48		head of leopard	ideo. or det. *pḥty* 'strength'
B49		forepart of lion	(1) ideo. *ḥꜣt* 'front'; (2) hence 3c. *ḥꜣt*
B50		hindpart of lion	2c. *pḥ*
B51		desert dog	det. dog, including the god Wepwawet
B52		dog com. standard	ideo. or det. *wp-wꜣwt* '(the god) Wepwawet'
B53		dog com. shrine	ideo. or det. *ỉnpw* '(the god) Anubis'
B54		head of dog	3c. *wsr*
B55		god with head of mythical animal	ideo. *sty* '(the god) Seth'
B56		hare	2c. *wn*
B57		pair of crocodiles	ideo. *ỉty* 'sovereign'
B58		mummified crocodile	ideo. *sbk* '(the god) Sobek'
B59		crocodile on shrine	ideo. *sbk* '(the god) Sobek', alternative for B58
B60		cobra	1c. *ḏ*
B61		horned viper	(1) 1c. *f*; (2) det.(?) *ỉt* 'father'
B62		E16 com. B61	3c. *ḫsf*, alternative for E16
B63		frog	det. frog, including the goddess Heket
B64		fish	det. or abb. fish
B65		oxyrhynchus fish	2c. *ẖꜣ*
B66		dung beetle	3c. *ḫpr*
B67		bee	abb. *bỉty* 'king'

§C. Signs depicting sky, earth, water or plants

C1		sun-disc	(1) det. sun, day, time; (2) ideo. *rꜥ* 'sun', '(the god) Re'
C2		sunrise above hills	2c. *ḫꜥ*
C3		canopy of the sky	(1) det. sky; (2) det. *ḥry* 'which is upon' (§60)
C4		C3 com. E4	det. night, darkness

C5		crescent moon	(1) det. moon, event based on lunar month; (2) ideo. *ỉꜥḥ* 'moon'
C6		star	(1) in *dwꜣ* 'adore'; (2) det. star; (3) det. *wnwt* 'priesthood'
C7		C5 com. C6	ideo. *ꜣbd* 'month' and related words
C8		half moon com. C6	ideo. half-month festival, reading uncertain (see p. 76)
C9		strip of land com. D4	(1) 2c. *tꜣ*; (2) det. in *ḏt* 'eternity'
C10		strip of land	alternative form of C9
C11		slope of hill	1c. *ḳ*
C12		valley between hills	2c. *ḏw*
C13		desert hills	(1) det. desert; (2) ideo. *ḫꜣst* 'foreign land'
C14		terraced slope	det. terrace
C15		ripple of water	1c. *n*
C16		group of ripples	(1) det. water, cleanse; (2) 2c. *mw*
C17		garden pool	1c. *š*
C18		pool with flowers	2c. *šꜣ*
C19		reeds	ideo. or det. *sḫt* 'countryside'
C20		reed	1c. *ỉ*
C21		pair of reeds	1c. *y*
C22		herb	(1) det. plant; (2) 2c. *ḥn*
C23		lotus	(1) 2c. *ḫꜣ*; (2) abb. *ḫꜣ* 'thousand', or units per thousand in counting
C24		clump of papyrus	2c. *ḥꜣ*
C25		sedge plant	(1) 2c. *sw*; (2) abb. *nsw* 'king'
C26		C25 com. D16	abb. *rḫ-nsw* 'king's adviser'
C27		flowering sedge	ideo. or det. *šmꜥ* 'Upper Egypt'
C28		pair of rushes	2c. *nn*
C29		tree	(1) det. tree; (2) 3c. *ỉꜣm, ỉmꜣ*
C30		tree branch	(1) det. *ḫt* 'wood' and related words; (2) hence 2c. *ḫt* ; (3) det. *pḳr* 'Poker', and *ḥꜣkr* 'Haker-rites'
C31		scented pod	(1) ideo. or det. *nḏm* 'sweet'; (2) hence 3c. *nḏm*
C32		scented rhysome	ideo. or det. *bnr* 'sweet'
C33		thorn	(1) ideo. or det. *spd* 'sharp, keen'; (2) hence 3c. *spd*

§D. *Other small signs*

D1	single stroke	(1) indicates word group or ideogram (§13); (2) abb. *wꜥ* 'one', or units of one in counting (§19)
D2	pair of strokes	1c. *y*, especially as the dual ending (§15)
D3	three strokes	(1) det. plurals (§8); (2) det. singular nouns which represent collections of individuals, e.g. *mšꜥ* 'expedition'
D4	grains of sand	det. mineral
D5	cattle hobble	abb. *mḏw* 'ten', or units of ten in counting (§19)
D6	irrigation canals	det. irrigated land
D7	crossed sticks	det. separate, cross, pass by
D8	burning charcoal with flames	(1) ideo. *km* 'black'; (2) hence 2c. *km*
D9	reed shelter	1c. *h*
D10	B1 as abbreviated for hieratic	1c. *w*, alternative for B1
D11	coil of rope	(1) det. rope; (2) abb. *š(n)t* 'hundred', or units per hundred in counting
D12	twisted cord	(1) 2c. *šs*; (2) hence abb. *šs* 'alabaster'
D13	twisted cord	2c. *šn*
D14	twisted cord (?)	det. *ḥbsw* 'clothing'
D15	reed mat or stool	1c. *p*
D16	placenta (?), ball of string (?)	1c. *ḫ*
D17	threshing-floor	2c. *sp*
D18	roads within enclosure	(1) ideo. *nwt* 'town'; (2) hence det. town, estate
D19	round loaf	det. *pꜣt* 'beginning of time', from a word *pꜣt* 'loaf' (similar writing)
D20	moon partly obscured	(1) 3c. *psḏ*; (2) by confusion, alternative for D19
D21	pustule	(1) det. *wt* in *ỉmy-wt*, title of Anubis; (2) det. scent, odour, disease; (3) abb. *ḥsb* 'count' and related words
D22	pustule with issue of fluid	det. scent, odour, disease, alternative for D21
D23	log stripped of bark	det. scent, scented wood
D24	bun	(1) 1c. *t*; (2) abb. *ỉt* in *ỉt-nṯr* 'god's father'
D25	small loaf	det. or abb. *t* 'bread'
D26	kiln	2c. *tꜣ*

D27		beer jug	det. or abb. *ḥnḳt* 'beer'
D28		basin (?)	det. *šnꜥw* 'magazine'
D29		well full of water	2c. *ḥm*
D30		bundle of flax	2c. *ḏr*
D31		jar-stand	(1) 1c. *g*; (2) ideo. *nst* 'throne'
D32		butcher's block	2c. *ẖr*
D33		pot	(1) 2c. *nw*; (2) 2c. *ỉn* (§49); (3) often as a graphic complement for *nḏ* (E15) and *ḳd* (E24).
D34		three pots	(1) 2c. *nw*, alternative for D33 at the end of a word; (2) 3c. *nnw* (?) in the name *nnwy*
D35		stone jug	3c. *ẖnm*
D36		part of steering-gear of boat (?)	(1) ideo. *ḥpt* 'steering oar'; (2) hence 2c. *ḥp*
D37		seal on necklace	ideo. or det. *ḫtm* 'seal' and related words
*		heart	see B45

§E. Other tall signs

E1		wooden staff	det. *ꜣryt* 'staff'
E2		throw-stick	(1) det. throw; (2) det. foreigner, enemy; (3) det. *ḳmꜣ* 'create'
E3		fuller's club	2c. *ḥm*
*		head of dog	see B54
E4		sceptre	3c. *wꜣs*
E5		sceptre with feather	ideo. *wꜣst* 'Thebes'
E6		sceptre with spiral shaft	3c. *ḏꜥm*
E7		standard with feather	ideo. *ỉmnt* 'the west' and related words
E8		totem	ideo. or det. *mnw* '(the god) Min'
E9		totem	ideo. *tꜣ-wr* 'the nome of Tawer'
E10		totem	ideo. or det. *ỉꜣt* 'office'
E11		crook	(1) ideo. *ḥḳꜣ* 'ruler'; (2) hence 3c. *ḥḳꜣ*
E12		crook with package	ideo. *šms* 'follow' and related words
E13		sceptre	(1) ideo. *ḫrp* 'control' and related words; (2) ideo. *sḫm* 'control' and related words
E14		stone mace	2c. *ḥḏ*

E15	unknown	2c. *nḏ,* usually accompanied by D33
E16	spindle	3c. *ḫsf*
E17	archaic dagger	in *tpy* 'which is upon' (§60)
E18	butcher's knife	2c. *nm*
E19	butcher's knife	alternative for E18
E20	arrow head	2c. *sn*
E21	target pierced by arrows	det. *sṯ(ỉ)* or *st(ỉ)* 'spear'
E22	cord wound on stick	2c. *wḏ*
E23	cord wound on stick	alternative for E22
E24	mortar float (?)	(1) ideo. or det. *ḳd* 'build' and related words; (2) hence 2c. *ḳd,* usually accompanied by D33
E25	notched palm	3c. *rnp*
E26	E25 com. D24	abb. *rnpt* 'year'
E27	pestle	2c. *tỉ*
E28	folded cloth	1c. *s*
E29	pennant	(1) ideo. *nṯr* 'god'; (2) hence 3c. *nṯr* in *snṯr* 'incense'
E30	E29 com. D32	ideo. *ẖrt-nṯr* 'cemetery'
E31	E29 com. C11 and D32	ideo. *ẖrt-nṯr* 'cemetery', alternative for E30
E32	three fox-skins	(1) 2c. *ms;* (2) a similar sign in *ꜣbt* 'family, household' is probably a writing of E71
E33	crossed planks	in *ỉmy* 'which is in' (§60)
E34	sandal strap	3c. *ꜥnḫ*
E35	twisted wick	1c. *ḥ*
E36	fibre swab	(1) 2c. *sk;* (2) 3c. *wꜣḥ*
E37	water pot	2c. *ḥs*
E38	rack of water pots	3c. *ḫnt*
E39	rack of water pots	alternative for E38
E40	water pot with issue of contents	ideo. or det. *ḳbḥw* 'libation water' and related words
E41	water pot in stand	alternative for E40
E42	ointment jar	det. or abb. *mrḥt* 'ointment'
E43	ointment jar	alternative for E42
E44	chisel	(1) 2c. *ꜣb;* (2) 2c. *mr*

E45	fire-drill	2c. *ḏꜣ*
E46	drill cutting bead	3c. *wbꜣ*, with a simpler variant
E47	palace facade	ideo. *ꜥḥ* 'palace'
E48	reed column	2c. *ḏd*
E49	wooden column	2c. *ꜥꜣ*
E50	pillar	(1) ideo. *ỉwn* 'pillar'; (2) hence 3c. *ỉwn*; (3) abb. *ỉwnw* 'the city of Heliopolis'
E51	shrine	ideo. or det. *sḥ* 'shrine'
E52	plan of estate	ideo. *ḥwt* 'enclosure, foundation'
E53	E52 com. D24 and F5	ideo. *nbt-ḥwt* '(the goddess) Nephthys'
E54	grain heap	ideo. or det. *šnwt* 'granary'
E55	fringed cloth	det. or abb. *mnḫt* 'linen'
E56	boat's mast	3c. *ꜥḥꜥ*
E57	oar	3c. *ḫrw*
E58	ship's sail	ideo. *ṯꜣw* 'breath'
E59	heart and windpipe	3c. *nfr*
E60	seat	(1) ideo. *st* 'place, seat'; (2) hence 2c. *st*; (3) hence (?) 2c. *ꜣs(t)* in *ꜣsỉr* '(the god) Osiris' and *ꜣst* '(the goddess) Isis'
E61	offering loaf	ideo. *dỉ* or *rdỉ* 'give', alternative for A41
E62	milk-jug within net	2c. *mỉ*
E63	lasso	2c. *wꜣ*
E64	brazier with flame	det. heat, cook
E65	bundle of reeds	2c. *ỉs*
E66	pieces of wood lashed together	2c. *rs*
E67	stylised balance	alternative for E66
E68	wall ornament	ideo. or det. *ḫkrt* 'diadem, ornament'
E69	writing equipment	ideo. *sẖ* 'scribe'
E70	royal crown	1c. *n* (from the 13th dynasty onwards)
E71	faience necklace	det. (?) *ꜣbt* 'family, household', alternative for F8

§F. Other broad signs

F1		papyrus roll	det. write, abstractions (§6)
F2		papyrus roll	earlier form of F1
F3		papyrus roll	alternative form for F1
F4		basket with handle	1c. *k*
F5		basket	2c. *nb*
F6		basin com. canopy	(1) det. festival; (2) abb. *ḥb* 'festival'
F7		alabaster basin	alternative for F6
F8		stylised bowl	(1) det. *ȝbw* 'the town of Elephantine'; (2) hence det. *ȝbt* 'family, household' (similar writing)
F9		loaf (for offering)	det. bread, offerings
F10		loaf (for offering)	alternative form of F9
F11		loaf on mat	ideo. *ḥtp* 'offer' and related words
F12		plan of house	(1) ideo. *pr* 'house, estate'; (2) hence 2c. *pr*; (3) det. building, location
F13		F12 com. D25, D27 and E57	abb. *prt-ḫrw* 'voice offering'
F14		laden offering table	det. *dbḥt-ḥtp* 'ritual offerings'
F15		door bolt	1c. *s*
F16		wooden column	alternative form of E49
F17		fence	3c. *šsp*
F18		lid or door	det. open
F19		stone block (?)	det. *ḳrs* 'bury', perhaps as alternative for F18
F20		coffin	det. coffin, burial
F21		carrying chair	ideo. *ȝsỉr* '(the god) Osiris' (see p. 41)
F22		statue plinth	3c. *mȝʿ*
F23		F22 com. F24	3c. *mȝʿ*
F24		sickle	2c. *mȝ*
F25		hoe	2c. *mr*
F26		plough	(1) 3c. *šnʿ* ; (2) 2c. *hb*
F27		adze on block	3c. *stp*
F28		knife or saw	ideo. or det. *sfṯw* or *sftw* 'butcher'
F29		knife-sharpener	3c. *sšm*

F30		harpoon	2c. *wꜥ*
F31		whip	2c. *mḥ*
F32		water-skin	2c. *šd*
F33		tethering rope	1c. *ṯ*
F34		fringed cloth com. E28	det. clothing
F35		weaver's comb (?)	alternative form of F34
F36		netting needle	2c. *ꜥḏ*
F37		girdle knot	(1) ideo. *ṯs(i̓)* 'tie' and related words; (2) hence 2c. *ṯs*
F38		pair of ribs (?)	(1) 2c. *gs*; (2) sound complement for *i̓m* or *m*
F39		vertebrae (?)	2c. *sꜣ*
F40		vertebrae (?)	later alternative for F39
F41		cattle hobble	2c. *sꜣ*
F42		road bordered by shrubs	ideo. or det. *wꜣt* 'road'
F43		canal	(1) 2c. *mr*, but read *m* in *mꜥḥꜥt* 'cenotaph'; (2) det. water
F44		irrigation canals	ideo. or det. *spꜣt* 'district'
F45		papyrus boat	det. papyrus boat
F46		papyrus (?) boat	det. *ḏꜣ(i̓)* 'ferry'
F47		ferry boat	det. *mḫnt* 'ferry-boat'
F48		boat with sail furled	det. boat, sail (downstream)
F49		boat under sail	det. sail (upstream)
F50		processional boat of Osiris	det. *nšmt* 'the Neshmet-boat of Osiris'
F51		processional boat of Osiris	alternative form of F50
F52		boat of Sokar	det. festivals for the god Soker
F53		sledge	2c. *tm*
F54		elephant tusk	(1) 2c. *bḥ*; (2) 2c. *ḥw*
F55		gaming board	2c. *mn*
F56		seal with necklace	ideo. *ḫtmty* 'seal-bearer', alternative for D38
F57		gold collar	(1) ideo. *nbw* 'gold'; (2) hence det. precious metal

Reference tables

Verb forms

The focus of this book is on reading actual monuments, rather than struggling through a morass of grammar. Nevertheless, a sizeable area of Egyptian grammar has also been covered. The reference tables provided here cover the grammar as presented in this book and are for quick reference and comparison.

Verb classes (§30)

Middle Egyptian verb-forms show differences in their writing according to the type of the verb. The following are the four basic verb classes:

STRONG VERBS	e.g.		*sḏm*	hear	stem does not usually show any alteration
DOUBLING VERBS	e.g.		*mꜣꜣ*	see	stem ends in a double consonant
WEAK VERBS	e.g.		*mr(i)*	love	stem ends with a 'weak' consonant, usually *-i*
EXTRA WEAK VERBS	e.g.		*rd(i)*	give	chiefly verbs with two or three weak consonants

Notes

i With weak verbs, the final *-i* is usually omitted in writing and therefore in transliteration, though for practical reasons we normally transliterate 'give' as *rdi*.

ii Extra weak verbs behave like ordinary weak verbs, but sometimes show additional features.

The infinitive (§31)

		INFINITIVE	
STRONG - no change		*sḏm*	hearing, to hear
DOUBLING - doubling		*mꜣꜣ*	seeing, to see
WEAK - end in *-t*		*mrt*	loving, to love
EXTRA WEAK - end in *-t*	 or 	*rdit/dit* (*r* optional)	giving, to give

The infinitive of strong verbs shows no specific writing, whereas weak verbs show a final *-t*.

Main tenses appearing in this book

The past tense (§§33 and 38)

		sḏm.n(=f)	
STRONG		*sḏm.n=f*	he heard
DOUBLING - no doubling		*mꜣ.n=f*	he saw
WEAK		*mr.n=f*	he loved
EXTRA WEAK		*(r)di.n=f* (*r* optional)	he gave

The present tense: general present sḏm(=f) and specific present ḥr sḏm (§§42–43)

		GENERAL PRESENT *sḏm(=f)*	
STRONG		*sḏm=f*	he hears
DOUBLING - doubling		*mꜣꜣ=f*	he sees
WEAK		*mr=f*	he loves
EXTRA WEAK		*di=f* (no *r*)	he gives

		SPECIFIC PRESENT *ḥr sḏm*	
STRONG		*ḥr sḏm*	is listening
DOUBLING		*ḥr mꜣꜣ*	is looking
WEAK		*ḥr mrt*	is loving
EXTRA WEAK		*ḥr rdit*	is giving

The specific present is made up of  *ḥr* followed by the infinitive.

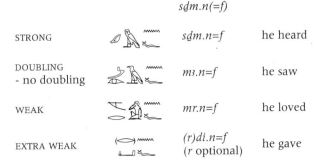

The future tense (wishes, requests, expectations): the future sḏm(=f) (§§55-57, §59)

	FUTURE *sḏm(=f)*		
STRONG		*sḏm=f*	may he hear
DOUBLING - no doubling		*m33=f*	may he see
WEAK	 or 	*mr=f* or *mry=f*	may he love
EXTRA WEAK		*di=f* (no *r*)	may he give
SPECIAL CASES		*iwt=f* (with extra *-t*)	may he come
		*int=f* (with extra *-t*)	may he bring

Notes

i The verb *m33* 'to see' also displays a form  *m3n=f*.

ii The weak verb form with  *-y* is most common in the first person.

iii Notice that the forms from the verbs 'to come' and 'to bring' show an extra *t* in the future *sḏm(=f)* form.

Negation (§§ 39 and 58)

The three principal tenses above are negated as follows:

	NEGATIONS		
PRESENT TENSE		*n sḏm.n=f*	he does not hear, he cannot hear
PAST TENSE		*n sḏm=f*	he did not hear
FUTURE TENSE		*nn sḏm=f*	may he not hear, he will not hear

The future is negated by adding the negation  *nn* to the future *sḏm(=f)* form. However, the present and past tense negatives display a most unusual apparent reversal – known as *Gunn's rule* – where ***n sḏm.n(=f)*** negates the present ***sḏm(=f)***, not the past *sḏm.n(=f)*, and ***n sḏm(=f)*** negates the past ***sḏm.n(=f)***, not the *sḏm(=f)*. In fact, the *sḏm(=f)* in this construction shows a special form:

n sḏm=f

STRONG VERBS	𓂜𓄔𓅓𓆑	*n sḏm=f*	he did not hear
DOUBLING VERBS - no doubling	𓂜𓌳𓁹𓅓𓆑	*n mꜣ=f*	he did not see
WEAK VERBS	𓂜𓌻𓂋𓀁𓆑	*n mr=f*	he did not love
EXTRA WEAK VERBS	𓂜𓂋𓂞𓆑	*n rdi͗=f* (with *r*)	he did not give

So, the present and past tense negatives are better thought of as constructions in their own right with their own grammar, rather than just as *sḏm(=f)* and *sḏm.n(=f)* with 𓂜 *n* stuck in front of them.

Specialised forms: the participles, relative forms and *sḏmty.fy*

The participles (§§46–51)

	PRESENT OR INCOMPLETE			PAST OR COMPLETE		
STRONG	𓄔𓅓	*sḏm*	(one) who hears	𓄔𓅓	*sḏm*	(one) who heard
DOUBLING	𓌳𓁹𓅓𓅓	*mꜣꜣ*	(one) who sees	𓌳𓁹𓅓	*mꜣ*	(one) who saw
WEAK	𓌻𓂋𓂋𓀁	*mrr*	(one) who loves	𓌻𓂋𓀁	*mr*	(one) who loved
EXTRA WEAK	𓂞𓂞	*dd* (no *r*)	(one) who gives	𓂋𓂞	*rdi͗* (with *r*)	(one) who gave

Participles also sometimes show a 𓅱 -*w* ending.

The relative forms (§§37 and 52)

	PRESENT OR INCOMPLETE			PAST OR COMPLETE		
STRONG	𓄔𓅓𓏏𓆑	*sḏmt=f*	what he hears	𓄔𓅓𓏏𓈖𓆑	*sḏmt.n=f*	what he heard
DOUBLING	𓌳𓁹𓅓𓅓𓏏𓆑	*mꜣꜣt=f*	what he sees	𓌳𓁹𓅓𓏏𓈖𓆑	*mꜣt.n=f*	what he saw
WEAK	𓌻𓂋𓂋𓏏𓀁𓆑	*mrrt=f*	what he loves	𓌻𓂋𓏏𓀁𓈖𓆑	*mrt.n=f*	what he loved
EXTRA WEAK	𓂞𓂞𓏏𓆑	*ddt=f*	what he gives	𓂋𓂞𓏏𓈖𓆑	*rdi͗t.n=f*	what he gave

Compare with the corresponding forms of the participles.

The relative forms here display the *-t* of feminine adjectival agreement. They can also occur in certain usages without the *-t* (i.e. with masculine adjectival agreement), though they still carry the same meaning of 'which someone does/did'. See §52.

The sḏmty.fy form (§§53-54, §59)

	sḏmty.fy	
STRONG VERBS	*sḏmty.fy*	(one) who may/will hear
DOUBLING VERBS	*m33ty.fy*	(one) who may/will see
WEAK VERBS	*šdty.fy*	(one) who may/will read
EXTRA WEAK VERBS	*rdìty.fy*	(one) who may/will give

Pronouns, nouns and adjectives

Suffix pronouns (§§33, 35, 36)

I	*=ì*	we	*=n*
you	*=k*	you (pl.)	*=ṯn* or *=tn*
you (fem.)	*=ṯ or =t*		
he/it	*=f*	they	*=sn*
she/it	*=s*		

Uses:

a. as the subject after a suffix-conjugation verb-form, such as *sḏm.n(=f)*
b. as the object after a preposition.
c. after auxiliaries.
d. as the possessor or genitive of nouns.

The suffix pronouns translate as the appropriate English pronoun, so or *=ì* translates as 'I' or 'me' or 'my' depending on English usage (and so on for the other pronouns). The use of 'I', 'you' etc. in the tables above and below is merely to point out the person or thing the pronoun refers to.

Dependent pronouns (§41)

I	or	*-wỉ* or *-w(ỉ)*	we		*-n*
you	or	*-ṯw* or *-tw*	you (pl.)	or	*-ṯn* or *-tn*
you (fem.)	or	*-ṯn* or *-tn*			
he/it	or	*-sw*	they	or	*-sn*
she/it	or	*-sy* or *-s(y)*	it, they		*-st*

-st is used for indefinite 'it' and generally as the dependent pronoun form for 'they/them'.

Uses:

a. Object of the verb (except the infinitive, which usually takes a suffix pronoun object).

b. After initial particles and the negation *nn*.

Independent pronouns (§49)

I	or	*ỉnk*	We		*ỉnn*
you		*ntk*	you (pl)	or	*ntṯn* or *nttn*
you (fem.)	or	*ntṯ* or *ntt*			
he/it		*ntf*	they	or	*ntsn*
she/it	or	*nts*			

Uses: As the subject of characterisations.

Nouns (§§8, 9, 15)

Nouns have a number (singular or plural) and a gender (masculine or feminine); the *-w* of the plural is often omitted in writing:

SG. MSC.	no special ending			*sn*	brother
SG. FEM.		*-t*		*snt*	sister
PL. MSC.		*-w*		*snw*	brothers
PL. FEM.		*-wt*		*snwt*	sisters

The dual ending msc. *-wy* and fem. *-ty* is common only with things which come in pairs:

	ꜥwy	arms		*tꜣwy*	the two lands (Upper and Lower Egypt)

Adjectives (§§10, 44-45)

Adjectives follow the noun they describe and agree with it in number and gender:

SG. MSC.		no special ending
SG. FEM.	𓏏	*-t*
PL. MSC.	𓅱	*-w*
PL. FEM.	𓏏	*-t*

The plural can also be written with the plural strokes, and the *-w* is often omitted in writing.

Adjectives can be used on their own as a noun, e.g.:

𓄤𓆑𓂋𓏏 *nfrt* the good (n.) from 𓄤𓆑𓂋 *nfr* good (adj.)

The genitive (§27)

Direct genitive: common only between closely connected words or in fixed expressions.

Indirect genitive: the two nouns are linked by forms of the 'genitival adjective' *n*:

	SINGULAR		PLURAL	
MASCULINE	𓈖	*n*	𓏌 or 𓈖	*nw* or *n*
FEMININE	𓈖𓏏	*nt*	𓈖𓏏	*nt*

Adjectives in -y (§60)

SG. MSC.	𓏭	*-y*	𓇋𓐛𓅓𓏭	*ỉmy*	who/which is in
SG. FEM.	𓏏	*-t*	𓇋𓐛𓅓𓏏	*ỉmt*	who/which is in
PL. MSC.	𓅱	*-w*	𓇋𓐛𓅓𓅱	*ỉmw*	who/which are in
PL. FEM.	𓏏	*-t*	𓇋𓐛𓅓𓏏	*ỉmt*	who/which are in

Egyptian–English vocabulary

Here, as in other Egyptian dictionaries, words are listed alphabetically in transliteration following the order set out in List 1 (the only exception being that the feminine ending *-t* is ignored, e.g. *s* 'man' and *st* 'woman' are listed together). In other words, the particular hieroglyphs used to write a word do not determine where it is listed. So to find a word, you need to know its reading in transliteration: if necessary, consult the various sign-lists. For example, imagine you come across the word but do not recognise its constituent signs. There are two stages in tracking down its meaning: (1) If you turn to List V beginning on p. 129, you will find (B62) has the reading *ḫsf*, whilst (F49) is not a sound-sign but a determinative for 'sail upstream'; so the reading of the whole word is *ḫsf*. (2) Returning to this vocabulary, you will find in the section headed *ḫ* that there are two words read *ḫsf* : 'repel' and 'travel upstream' (see p. 158). Of course, the determinative indicates that the second of these is the correct meaning, although, more often than not, the context in which the word occurs will also help you decide which of the two is correct. Although the hieroglyphic writings given in this list are representative of what you may find, it is not possible to list all of the ways in which a word could be written (see §14 again, if you are not yet sure about this). The following abbreviations have been used here: (a.) adjective; (n.) noun; (v.) strong verb; (w.v.) weak verb; (f.) feminine; (pl.) plural.

ꜣ

ꜣw (a.) long; joyful

ꜣbt (n.) family, household

ꜣbd (n.) month; monthly festival

ꜣbḏw Abydos (place name)

ꜣpd (n.) bird

ꜣryt (n.) staff

ꜣḫ (v.) become an akh-spirit; be useful

(n.) akh-spirit

ꜣst (the goddess) Isis (see p. 70)

ꜣsꞽr (the god) Osiris; possibly read *wsꞽr*

ꞽ

=ꞽ I, me, my (suffix pronoun, p. 148)

ꞽ O! (interjection) (§54a)

ꞽꜣt (n.) office, function

ꞽꜣ(w) (n.) praise, adoration

ꞽꜣw (a.) old; (n.) old age

ꞽꞽ or *ꞽy(ꞽ)* (w.v.) come

ỉỉw welcome see also *ỉw(ỉ)*

ỉꜥḥ (n.) moon

ỉw see §34

ỉw(ỉ) (w.v.) come

ỉw welcome see also *ỉy(ỉ)*

ỉw(ỉ) (w.v.) be boatless

ỉww (n.) boatless person

ỉwꜣ (n.) ox

ỉwꜣ(w) (n.) cattle

ỉwỉt (n.) wrongdoing

ỉwn (n.) pillar.

ỉwnw Heliopolis (place-name)

ỉwrỉ Iuri (name)

ỉb (n.) heart; see also *ḫrt-ỉb, st-ỉb*

ỉb(ỉ) (w.v.) be thirsty

ỉb thirsty person

ỉp (v.) count, inspect

ỉmꜣ (a.) charming, gracious (the writing indicates the reading has become *ỉꜣm* or *ỉm*)

ỉmꜣḫ (n.) reverence

or or *ỉmꜣḫy* or *ỉmꜣḫw* (n.) revered one.

or *ỉmy* (a.) who/which is in (§60)

ỉmy-wt 'the one who is in the *wt*', i.e. Anubis (title)

ỉmy-ḫnt chamberlain (title)

ỉmn (the god) Amun

ỉmn-m-ḥꜣt Amenemhet (name)

ỉmn-rꜥ (the god) Amun-Re

ỉmny Ameny (name)

ỉmnt (n.) west

ỉmnty (a.) western; for *ỉmntw* people of the west, see *ḫnt*

ỉmstỉ (the god) Imseti, one of the sons of Horus.

ỉn by (§28); 'it is' (§51)

ỉn(ỉ) (w.v.) bring

ỉnw (n.) produce, gifts

ỉn-ḥrt-nḫt Inhuretnakht (name)

ỉnpw (the god) Anubis

ỉnk I (independent pronoun, §49)

ỉntf Intef (name)

ỉr(ỉ) (w.v.) do, make; plus many idomatic meanings

ỉr-n made by, i.e. born of

ỉry (a.) relating to (§60)

ỉry (n.) keeper

ỉry-nfr-ḥꜣt (title) keeper of the king's diadem

ỉs (n.) tomb

ỉḳr (a.) excellent, effective, astute

ỉḳdw (n.) builder; see *ḳd*

or *ỉt* (n.) father

ỉt(w) (n.) forefathers

ỉt-nṯr god's father (title)

ỉty (n.) sovereign

ỉty Ity (name)

ỉtn (n.) sun-disc; (the god) Aten

 or  *iṯ(i)* (w.v.) seize (the latter writing indicates the reading has become *iṯ*)

 ꜥ

 *ꜥ* (n.) arm; note 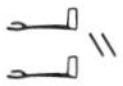 *ꜥwy* arms; see also *ẖry-ꜥ*, *st-ꜥ*, *tp-ꜥ*

 *ꜥꜣ* (a.) great

 *ꜥꜣ(w)* (n.) the great (in society)

 *ꜥꜣt* in *n-ꜥꜣt-n* because of

 *ꜥmꜥꜣ* (v.) throw (a throw-stick)

 *ꜥnḫ* (v.) live; (n.) life

 *ꜥnḫ ḏt* living for all time

ꜥnḫw (n.) the living

ꜥnḫt nṯr im on which a god lives (§26)

 *di ꜥnḫ* given life

 *ꜥnḫ-n-nwt* (n.) local soldier

 *ꜥḥ* (n.) palace

ꜥḥꜣ (v.) fight; (n.) fighting

ꜥḥꜥ (v.) stand

ꜥḫnwty variant form of *ꜥẖnwty*

ꜥẖnwty (n.) chamber; *m-r ꜥẖnwty* overseer of the chamber (title)

 *ꜥḳyt* (n.) entering maid

 *w*

 or  *wꜣt* (n.) road, way

 or  *wꜣst* Thebes (place-name)

 *wꜣg* (n.) the Wag-festival

 or  *-wi* I, me (dependent pronoun, p. 149)

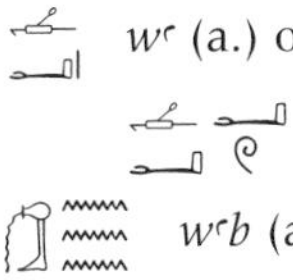 *wꜥ* (a.) one, alone

wꜥꜥw (n.) privacy

wꜥb (a.) pure

 *wꜥb* (n.) pure one, i.e. *wꜥb*-priest

 or  *wbꜣ* (n.) cup-bearer

 *wbꜣt* (fem.) cup-bearer

 *wp(i)* (w.v.) open, separate

 *wp-wꜣwt* (the god) Wepwawet

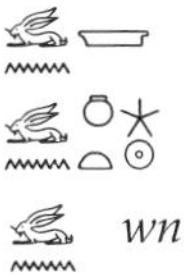 *wn* (v.) open

wnwt (n.) priesthood

wnn (v.) be, exist; *n-wn-mꜣꜥ* truly, truthfully.

 *wnn-nfr* (the god) Wenennefer, i.e. Osiris

 *wr* (a.) great, important

wr(w) (n.) the great (in society)

wrt (n.) the great bark

 *wḥm* (v.) repeat; (n.) reporter, herald (title)

 *wsr* (a.) powerful

 *wsrt* Wosret (name), literally 'powerful one' and may be used as a designation for female deities

 *wt* see *imy*

wḏ (v.) order; (n.) order

wḏꜣ (v.) set out, proceed

 *b*

 or  *bꜣ* (n.) ba-spirit

bꜣ-mkt Bameket (name)

bꜣḥ see *m-bꜣḥ*

bꜣk (n.) servant (see p. 101)

bỉn (a.) bad

or *bỉty* (n.) king

bnr (a.) pleasant

bt Bet (name)

p

pt (n.) sky

pꜣt (n.) antiquity, beginning of time

pw it is, this is

pf that; (fem.) *tf*, (pl.) *nf*.

pn this; (fem.) *tn*, (pl.) *nn*.

pr (n.) estate

pr-ꜥꜣ (n.) palace

m-r pr overseer of an estate, steward; see also *nbt-pr*, *r-pr*

pr(ỉ) (w.v.) go out

prt (n.) going out, procession

prt-ḫrw (n.) voice-offering

or *pḥty* (a.) strength

pḳr Poker (place-name); see also *r-pḳr*

or *ptr* (v.) observe, view

ptḥ (the god) Ptah

ptḥ-ḥtp Ptahhotep (name)

f

=f he, him, his (suffix pronoun, p. 148)

m

m in

m-bꜣḥ in the presence of

or *m-m* among

or *m-r* (n.) overseer; for specific titles, e.g. *m-r pr,* see the second element

mꜣꜣ (v.) see, look at

mꜣỉ-n-ḥr Maienhor (name)

mꜣꜥ (v.) present, guide

or *mꜣꜥ* (v.) be true, right, proper; (a.) true; for *n-wn-mꜣꜥ* see *wn*

mꜣꜥ-ḫrw (a.) true of voice, justified; (v.) be justified

or *mꜣꜥt* (n.) what is proper, i.e. truth, harmony; (the goddess) Maat, often written

mỉ as, like

or *mỉty* (n.) equal, peer

mꜥḥꜥt (n.) cenotaph, tomb

mꜥḳ (v.) roast

mw (n.) water

mwt (n.) mother

mnꜥt (n.) wet-nurse

mnw dedication, monument (see p. 126)

mnw (the god) Min

mnw-nfr Minnefer (name)

or *mnḫt* (n.) linen

mnṯw (the god) Montju

mnṯw-ḥtp Mentjuhotep (name)

mr(i) (w.v.) want, love

or *mrḥt* (n.) oil, unguent

mrs Meres (name)

mrti Merti (name)

mḫnt (n.) ferry

ms (v.) bring, present

m-sꜣ=f Emsaf (name)

ms(i) (w.v.) give birth

ms-n born of

msw (n.) offspring

msḏ(i) (w.v.) hate

mšꜥ (n.) expedition, army

m-r mšꜥ wr general-in-chief

mdḥw Medhu (name)

n

=n we, us, our (suffix pronoun, p. 148), *-n* we, us (dependent pronoun, p. 149)

n to, for; for negative *n* (§39); for *n-ꜥꜣt-n* see *ꜥꜣ*; for *n-wn-mꜣꜥ* see *wn*

n of (§27); (f.) *nt;* (pl.) *nw*

negative *n* (§39)

n sp never

nis (v.) call out, summon

nw see *n*

nwt (the goddess) Nut

nwt (n.) town, city; see also *nṯr*

nb all, every (§16)

nb (n.) possessor, lord (§16, §25)

nbt (n.) possessor (f.), lady

nbt pr (n.) lady of the house, mistress of the estate, i.e. woman of high status

nb(=i)-pw-snwsrt Nebipusenusret (name)

or *nbt-ḥwt* (the goddess) Nephthys

nbw (n.) gold

n-ptḥ-kꜣw Niptahkau (name)

nf see *pf*

nfr (a.) perfect, good, wonderful, beautiful

nfrw (n.) perfection, splendour

or *nmtt* (n.) step, formal journey

nn see *pn*

nn without; future negation (§58)

nnwy Nenwy (name)

or *nḥḥ* (n.) (for) eternity

nḫnt (n.) youth

nḫt (a.) strong, vigorous

nḫti Nakhti (name)

nḫt-ꜥnḫ Nakhtankh (name)

nsw (n.) king (§23)

nsw-bity king of the dualities, king of Upper and Lower Egypt (royal title)

nšt (n.) hairdresser

nšmt (n.) Neshmet-bark, the processional boat of Osiris

ngꜣw (n.) long-horned bull

nt-nbw Netnebu (name)

nṯr (n) god

nṯrw nwtw town-gods

nṯr nfr the perfect god (royal title) (§17)

ndyt Nedyet (place-name)

nḏ (v.) protect

nḏm (a.) sweet

nḏs (a.) small

nḏs (n.) person, individual

nḏs(w) (n.) the lowly

r

r towards, at; more than (p, 81); in order to (p. 84); for words compounded with *r* see under the second element, e.g. *r-ḥꜣt*, etc.

r (n.) mouth

r-pr (n.) temple complex

r-pḳr Ro-Poker (place-name); see also *pḳr*

or *rʿ* (n.) day; sun; (the god) Ra or Re

or *rm(w)* (n.) fish

rmṯ (n.) people

rn (n.) name

rnpt (n.) year

rnpt-sp (n.) regnal year

tp-rnpt (n.) festival of the beginning of the lunar year

rrwt Rerut (name)

rḫ (v.) know, learn

or *rḫ-nsw* king's adviser, king's confidant (title)

rḫty (n.) washerman

rd or *rwd* (n.) terrace

or *rd(i)* (w.v.) give, put; cause (§40)

rdwy (n.) legs, feet

h

hꜣ(i) (w.v.) descend

hꜣb (v.) send

hꜣkr (n.) Haker-rites (at Abydos)

hi (n.) husband

hbny (n.) ebony

hnw (n.) jubilation

hrw (n.) day, daytime

ẖrt-hrw daily course

ḥ

ḥꜣt (n.) front

r-ḥꜣt before

ẖr-ḥꜣt before

ḥꜣy (a.) naked

(n.) naked person

ḥꜣty-ʿ (n.) governor, mayor

ḥʿpy (n.) Nile inundation (often personified as the god Hapy)

ḥwt (n.) enclosure, foundation

ḥwt-nṯr (n.) temple

ḥwt-ḥr (the goddess) Hathor

ḥw(ỉ) (w.v.) beat

ḥwt (n.) beating

ḥwỉ Hui (name)

or *ḥb* (n.) festival

ḥbs (v.) clothe

ḥbsw (n.) clothing

ḥpt (n.) oar

ḥpy (the god) Hapy, i.e. one of the sons of Horus

ḥm (n.) person (§19)

ḥm-nṯr (n.) *ḥm*-priest

ḥmt-nṯr (f.) *ḥm*-priestess

ḥm-kꜣ (n.) *ka*-priest

ḥmt (n.) wife

ḥnʿ together with

or *ḥnḳt* (n.) beer (§23)

ḥr (the god) Horus; as king's name (§17)

ḥr (n.) face

ḥr on, at; because of; usually written before suffixes; as verbal auxiliary (§42)

ḥry (a) who/which is upon (§60)

ḥry-pr (n.) domestic servant

ḥrt-pr (fem.) domestic servant

or *ḥry-sštꜣ* (n.) master of secrets

ḥry-tp (n.) chief, superior

see *nḥḥ*

ḥs(ỉ) (w.v.) praise

ḥst (n.) favour

ḥsb (n.) counter

ḥsmn (n.) amethyst

ḥḳt (the goddess) Heket

ḥḳꜣ (v.) rule

ḥḳꜣ (n.) ruler

ḥḳr (v.) hunger

(n.) hungry person

ḥtp (v.) content, satisfy, rest, be content; (n.) peace, satisfaction; (n.) offering; (n.) altar; Hetep (name)

ḥtp-nṯr (n.) divine offerings

ḥtpt offerings

ḥtp dỉ nsw (n.) an offering which the king gives (§26)

ḫ

ḫt (n.) thing, things

ḫꜣ (n.) thousand

ḫw Khu (name)

ḫwyt Khuyt (name)

ḫw-n-bỉk Khuenbik (name)

ḫpt (n.) death

ḫpr (v.) become; (n.) form, being

ḫpš (n.) foreleg, strong arm

ḫfty (n.) enemy

ḫnm (v.) gladden

ḫnms (n.) friend

ḫnt in front

ḫnty (a.) who/which is in front, foremost (§60)

ḫnty-ỉmntw Khentyimentu, i.e. 'foremost of the westerners' (name of Osiris) *ḫnty sḥ-nṯr* 'the one in front at the god's booth' (epithet of Anubis)

see *imy-ḫnt*

ḫntyt Khentyt (place-name)

ḫnt-ḫty-ḥtp Khenetkhetyhetep (name)

ḫr before, in front of

ḫr (v.) fall

ḫrt-ib (n.) wish, preference; see *st*

ḫrw (n.) voice; for *mꜣꜥ-ḫrw* see *mꜣꜥ*

ḫrp (v.) control; director (title)

ḫsf (v.) repel, ward off

ḫsf(w) (w.v.) travel upstream, travel south; see also *ḫd(i)*

ḫtm (n.) seal

ḫtmw ẖry-ꜥ seal-bearer, assistant (title)

ḫtmty-bity seal-bearer of the king (title)

m-r ḫtmt treasurer (title)

ḫd(i) (w.v.) travel north, travel downstream; see also *ḫsf(w)*

ẖ

ẖnw (n.) interior; the interior, i.e. the palace

r-ẖnw inside

ẖnm (v.) join; (a.) united with (*m*)

ẖnmw (the god) Khnum

ẖr under, carrying

ẖry (a.) who/which is under, carrying (§60)

ẖry-ꜥ (n.) deputy, assistant;

ẖry-ḥbt (n.) lector-priest

ẖry-tp chamberlain (title)

ẖrt (n.) share, duty

ẖrt-hrw (n.) daily course

or *ẖrt-nṯr* (n.) cemetery

ẖrd (n.) child

ẖkrt-nsw lady-in-waiting (title)

or *s*

or =*s* she, her (suffix pronoun, p. 148)

s (n.) man

st (n.) woman

-*st* she, her, it, they (dependent pronoun, p. 149)

st (n.) place, position, status

st-ib (n.) affection, intimacy

st-ꜥ (n.) ability

st-ḫrt-ib (n.) confidence

m-r st overseer of the storehouse (title)

see *smyt* (§23)

sꜣ (n.) son

sꜣt (n.) daughter

sꜣ-imn Saamun (name)

sꜣt-wsrt Satwosret (name)

sꜣ-mnḫt Samenkhet (name)

sꜣt-mnṯw Satmontju (name)

sꜣ-rnnwtt Sarenenutet (name)

sꜣ-ḥwt-ḥr Sahathor (name)

sꜣ-ḫnt-ḫty Sakhentkhety (name)

sꜣt-ḫnt-ḫtỉ Satkhentkheti (name)

sꜣt-sbk Satsobek (name)

sꜣwtyt Sautyt (name)

sꜣḫ (v.) transform into an akh-spirit, transfigure

-sy she, her, it (dependent pronoun, p. 149)

sꜥꜣ (v.) promote, advance

sꜥnḫ (v.) perpetuate (name)

or *-sw* he, him (dependent pronoun, p. 149)

or *swꜣ* (v.) pass by, surpass

swꜥb (v.) decorate

swḏ (v.) bequeath

or *sbỉ* (v.) rebel; *sbỉ* (n.) rebel

sbk (the god) Sobek

sp (n.) moment, deed; for *n sp* see *n*; for *rnpt-sp* see *rnpt*

spꜣt (n.) district.

sp(ỉ) (w.v.) bind (together)

spḥ (v.) lassoo

spdt (the goddess) Sothis

sfṯw or *sftw* (n.) butcher

smỉ (w.v.) report; (n.) report

smyt (n.) desert (see §23)

smr (n.) courtier, royal companion

smr wꜥt(y) (n.) sole companion

smḥ (n.) papyrus skiff

smsw (a.) elder, eldest

or *=sn* they, them, their (suffix pronoun, p. 148); *-sn* they, them (dependent pronoun, p. 149)

sn (n.) brother

snt (n.) sister

snw snwt (n.) siblings, brothers and sisters

sn (v.) kiss

s-n-wsrt Senwosret (name)

snb (n.) health; (a.) healthy

snbỉ Senbi (name)

snfr (v.) improve

snt Senet (name)

snṯr (n.) incense

sr (n.) official

srw (n.) goose

srḫ (v.) complain about, accuse

sḥ in *ḫnty sḥ-nṯr*, see under *ḫnt*

sḥtp (v.) satisfy; see also *ḥtp*

sḥtp-ỉb Sehetepib (name)

sḫt (n.) countryside

sḫmḫ-ỉb (n.) delight

sḫnt (v.) promote, augment

sḫr (v.) fell, overturn

sḫr (n.) conduct, plan

sḫsf (v.) (keep at a) distance

sẖ (n.) scribe; possibly to be read *sš*

sšm (n.) procedure, conduct

sštꜣ (a.) secret; see also *ḥry-sštꜣ*

sḳbḥ (v.) relax, calm down

sḳd(i) (w.v.) travel, sail

skr (the god) Soker

st (n.) scent; originally *sty*

st(i) (w.v.) shoot, spear

stp (v.) choose; (a.) chosen

sḏꜣ (v.) travel, depart

sḏm (v.) hear, listen; the alternative indicates that the reading had become *sdm*

sḏrt (n.) vigil

š

šw (v.) be free from (*m*)

šw (the god) Shu

špsy (a.) dignified, wealthy

šps-nsw (n.) dignitary of the king

špswt (n.) dignity

špss (n.) wealth, dignity

šmꜥ (n.) Upper Egypt

šms (v.) follow

šmsw (n.) follower, attendant

šmsw (n.) following

šn (divine epithet) in Hor-*šn*, a name of Horus

šnyt (n.) entourage

šnwt (n.) granary

or *šnꜥ* or *šnꜥw* (n.) magazine, provisioning area

or *šs* (n.) alabaster (calcite)

šsp (v.) receive

šd(i) (w.v.) read, recite

ḳ

ḳis Qis (Cusae) (place-name)

ḳbw Kebu (name)

ḳbḥ-snw=f (the god) Qebehsenuf, i.e. one of the sons of Horus

or *ḳmꜣ* (v.) create

ḳrs (v.) bury

ḳrst burial

ḳd (v.) build; see also *iḳdw*

k

=k you, your (suffix pronoun, p. 148)

kꜣ (n.) ka-spirit

or *kꜣ* (n.) ox, bull

ky Key (name)

g

gb (the god) Geb

gm(i) (w.v.) find

grḥ (n.) night

t

=t you, your (f.) (see *=ṯ*)

or *t* (n.) bread

tꜣ (n.) land

tꜣwy (n.) the two lands, i.e. Upper and Lower Egypt

tꜣ-wr the nome of Thinis (place-name)

-tw you (see *-ṯw*)

tp (n.) head

tp-ꜥ (n.) ancestor

(for *ḥry-tp* see *ḥry*; for *ẖry-tp* see *ẖry*; for *tp-rnpt* see *rnpt*)

or *tpy* (a.) who/which is upon, chief (§60)

tpy ḏw=f 'the one who is upon his mountain' (title of Anubis)

tf see *pf*

tfnt (the goddess) Tefenet

tn see *pn*

=tn, -tn you, your (pl.) (see *=ṯn, -ṯn*)

ṯ

=ṯ you, your (f.) (suffix pronoun, p. 148)

ṯꜣw (n.) breath, wind

ṯꜣw Tjau (name)

=ṯn you, your (pl.) (suffix pronoun, p. 148);
-ṯn you (pl.) (dependent pronoun, p. 149)

-ṯw you (dependent pronoun, p. 149)

ṯs(ỉ) (w.v.) tie, knot, assign

ṯsw (n.) sandbank

d

or *d(ỉ)* (w.v.) give; see *rd(ỉ)*

ddt Dedet (name)

dwꜣ (v.) adore

or *dwꜣ-mwt=f* (the god) Duamutef, one of the sons of Horus

dbỉ Debi (name)

dbḥt-ḥtp (n.) required offerings

dpt (n.) boat

ḏ

ḏt (n.) (for) all time, enduringly; see also under *ꜥnḫ*

ḏꜣt (n.) wrongdoing

ḏꜣ(ỉ) (w.v.) cross, ferry

ḏꜣt (n.) boat-journey

ḏꜥm (n.) electrum

ḏw (n.) mountain; for *tpy ḏw=f* see *tpy*

ḏws (v.) denounce

or *ḏf(ꜣw)* (n.) provisions

ḏfꜣ-ḥꜥpy Djefahapy (name)

ḏḥwty (the god) Thoth

ḏḥwtt (n.) the festival of Thoth

ḏr since

ḏr-ntt because

ḏs self; used in conjunction with suffix pronoun, *ḏs=ỉ* 'myself', etc

ḏsr (v.) separate, clear; (a.) sacred

tꜣ ḏsr the sacred land (place-name)

ḏd (v.) say, speak

or *ḏdw* Djedu (place-name)

Reading uncertain

?-nt (n.) half-month festival, perhaps read *mḏdỉnt* or *smdt* (see p. 76)

Key to the exercises

Chapter 1

1.1 Kings' names:

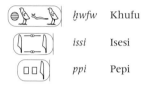

	*ḫwfw*	Khufu
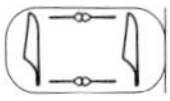	*ỉssỉ*	Isesi
	*ppỉ*	Pepi

1.2 Words from the roasting scene:

	*mꜥḳ*		*srw*

1.3 Gods' names:

	*ỉnpw*		*ḥḳt*
	*ptḥ*		*sbk*
	*rꜥ*		*skr*
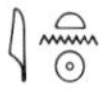	*ỉtn*		

1.4 Transliterating words:

	*nḏs*		*rn*
	*ḥb*		*bỉn*
	*ꜣpd*		*ỉḳr*
	*ꜥmꜥꜣ*		*pḳr*
	*ꜣryt*		*ḫd*
	*pt*		*rm*
	*ḥbs*	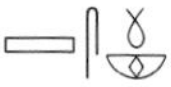	*šs*
	*ḫpš*		*stt*

1.5 Writing out words in hieroglyphs:

ḫr	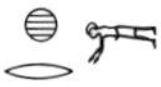	*ḫtm*	
sr		*ḳrst*	

1.6 Translation:

a.	*nḏs ỉḳr*	the/an astute individual
b.	*sḫr ỉḳr*	the/an excellent plan
c.	*ḥnꜥ snbỉ*	with Senbi
d.	*r pḳr*	to Poker

1.7 Translating the offering scene:

ḫpš n kꜣ n snbỉ mꜣꜥ-ḫrw A foreleg for the ka of Senbi, the justified.

1.8 Study exercise: A fishing and fowling scene:

Above scene on left:
stt rm(w) ỉn snbỉ mꜣꜥ-ḫrw
Spearing the fish by Senbi, the justified.

Above scene on right
ꜥmꜥꜣ r ꜣpd(w) ỉn snbỉ mꜣꜥ-ḫrw
Throwing at the birds by Senbi, the justified.

Chapter 2

2.2 Words:

	*sꜣ*	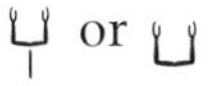	*kꜣ*		
	*wꜣt*		*mr*		
	*smr*		*wp*		
	*ꜣbḏw*		*ḏdw*		
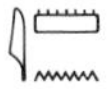	*ỉmn*		*ẖnmw*		*wp-wꜣwt*

2.4 Expressions:

a.  *nṯr ꜥꜣ* great god

b.  *ḫt nbt nfrt wꜥbt* everything good and pure

2.6 Dating:

a. *rnpt-sp 25 ḫr ḥm (n) nṯr nfr nb tꜣwy* — Regnal year 25 under the person of the perfect god, the lord of the two lands
n-mꜣꜥt-rꜥ dỉ ꜥnḫ mỉ rꜥ ḏt — Nimaatre, given life like Re enduringly.

b. *rnpt-sp 14 ḫr ḥm n nsw-bỉty* — Regnal year 14 under the person of the king of Upper and Lower Egypt
ḫpr-kꜣ-rꜥ ꜥnḫ ḏt — Kheperkare, living enduringly.

c. *rnpt-sp 13 ḫr ḥm n nsw-bỉty* — Regnal year 13 under the person of the king of Upper and Lower Egypt
nbw-kꜣw-rꜥ dỉ ꜥnḫ ḏt r nḥḥ — Nubkaure, given life enduringly and repeatedly.

2.7 Study exercise: Middle Kingdom kings of the 12th dynasty:

The order of the first cartouche names should be as follows:

sḥtp-ỉb-rꜥ	(Amenemhet I)	*ḫꜥ-kꜣw-rꜥ*	(Senwosret III)
ḫpr-kꜣ-rꜥ	(Senwosret I)	*n-mꜣꜥt-rꜥ*	(Amenemhet III)
nbw-kꜣw-rꜥ	(Amenemhet II)	*mꜣꜥ-ḫrw-rꜥ*	(Amenemhet IV)
ḫꜥ-ḫpr-rꜥ	(Senwosret II)	*sbk-kꜣ-rꜥ*	(Nefrusobek)

2.8 Study exercise: New Kingdom pharaohs:

The New Kingdom pharaohs listed are:

nb-pḥty-rꜥ	*ỉꜥḥ-ms*	Ahmose
ḏsr-kꜣ-rꜥ	*ỉmn-ḥtp*	Amenhotep I
ꜥꜣ-ḫpr-kꜣ-rꜥ	*ḏḥwty-ms*	Thutmose I
ꜥꜣ-ḫpr-n-rꜥ	*ḏḥwty-ms*	Thutmose II
mꜣꜥt-kꜣ-rꜥ	*ḥꜣt-špswt ẖnmt-ỉmn*	Hatshepsut
mn-ḫpr-rꜥ	*ḏḥwty-ms*	Thutmose III
ꜥꜣ-ḫprw-rꜥ	*ỉmn-ḥtp ḥḳꜣ-ỉwnw*	Amenhotep II
mn-ḫprw-rꜥ	*ḏḥwty-ms*	Thutmose IV
nb-mꜣꜥt-rꜥ	*ỉmn-ḥtp ḥḳꜣ-wꜣst*	Amenhotep III
nfr-ḫprw-rꜥ wꜥ-n-rꜥ	*ꜣḫ-n-ỉtn*	Akhenaten
nb-ḫprw-rꜥ	*twt-ꜥnḫ-ỉmn ḥḳꜣ-ỉwnw-šmꜥ*	Tutankhamun

ḏsr-ḫprw-rꜥ stp-n-rꜥ	*ḥr-m-ḥb mry-imn*	Horemheb
mn-pḥty-rꜥ	*rꜥ-ms-sw*	Ramesses I
mn-mꜣꜥt-rꜥ	*sty mry-n-ptḥ*	Seti I
wsr-mꜣꜥt-rꜥ stp-n-rꜥ	*rꜥ-ms-sw mry-imn*	Ramesses II
wsr-mꜣꜥt-rꜥ mry-imn	*rꜥ-ms-s(w) ḥkꜣ-iwnw*	Ramesses III

2.9 Study exercise: BM EA 117

The missing pharaohs are all the pharaohs of the 13th–17th dynasties inclusive, and within the 18th dynasty, Hatshepsut, Akhenaten and Tutankhamun (as well as the other Amarna pharaohs, Ay and the shadowy figure of Neferneferuaten/Smenkhkare).

Chapter 3

3.2 Words:

 *wr*  *imny*

3.3 Gods' names:

 *ḫnty-imntw*  *wnn-nfr*

3.4 Titles

 *m-r ꜥḫnwty*  *smr-wꜥty*

3.6 The offering formula from BM EA 162:

ḥtp-di-nsw	An offering which the king gives/places
ḥr ꜣsir ḫnty-imntw	before Osiris-Khentyimentu,
[nṯr ꜥꜣ nb] ꜣbḏw	[great god, lord] of Abydos,
m s(w)t=f nbt nfrt wꜥbt	in all his good and pure places,
di=f prt-ḫrw	so that he may give a voice offering
m t m ḥnḳt	in bread and in beer
m kꜣ ꜣpd m ḫt nb(t) nfrt	in ox and fowl and everything good
n kꜣ n imꜣḫw ḫr nṯr ꜥꜣ	for the ka of the revered one before the great god,
m-r mšꜥ wr imny	the general-in-chief Ameny,
ir-n ḳbw mꜣꜥ-ḫrw	born of Kebu, the justified.

3.7 Offering table scene:

dbḥt-ḥtp	The required offerings:
ḫꜣ(w) kꜣ ꜣpd ḫt nbt nfrt wꜥbt	thousands of ox and fowl and everything good and pure
n kꜣ n imꜣḫy	for the ka of the revered one,
ḥꜣty-ꜥ snbi mꜣꜥ-ḫrw	the governor Senbi, the justified.

3.8 Study exercise: BM EA 587

ḥtp-di-nsw	An offering which the king gives
ꜣsir nb ḏdw nṯr ꜥꜣ nb ꜣbḏw	to Osiris, lord of Djedu, great god, lord of Abydos,
prt-ḫrw	a voice offering of
t ḥnḳt kꜣ ꜣpd šs mnḫt	bread and beer, ox and fowl, alabaster and linen,
ḫt nbt nfrt wꜥbt	and everything good and pure
ꜥnḫt nṯr im	on which a god lives
n kꜣ n imꜣḫ(w)	for the ka of the revered one,
m-r ꜥḫnw(ty) imn-m-ḥꜣt mꜣꜥ-ḫrw	the overseer of the chamber Amenemhet, the justified.

3.9 Study exercise: BM EA 585

ḥtp-di-nsw	An offering which the king gives
ꜣsir nb ḏdw nṯr ꜥꜣ nb ꜣbḏw	to Osiris, lord of Djedu, great god, lord of Abydos,
di=f ḫꜣ m	so that he may give 1000 of
t ḥnḳt kꜣ ꜣpd šs mnḫt	bread and beer, ox and fowl, alabaster and linen,
ḫt nbt ꜥnḫt nṯr im	and everything on which a god lives
n kꜣ n imꜣḫy	for the ka of the revered one,
dd ḥtp-nṯr n nṯrw	the offering-giver to the gods,
ḥsb-šnwty m-r pr	the counter of the double granaries and steward
sꜣ-rnnwtt mꜣꜥ-ḫrw	Sarenenutet, the justified,
ms-n bꜣ-mkt	born of Bameket.

Chapter 4

Labels to the map of Abydos on p. 55:

rwd n nṯr ꜥꜣ	the terrace of the great god.
ḥwt-nṯr nt ꜣsir ḫnty-imntw	the temple of Osiris-Khentyimentu.
pḳr	Poker
tꜣ ḏsr	sacred land

4.2 Words:

	*snt*		*ḥmt*
	*dwꜣ*		*sn*
	*sn*		*wḥm*

4.3 Translation:

Meir II, pl. 4:	*spḫ ngꜣw* Lassooing the long-horned bull
Meir I, pl. 11:	*wpt kꜣ(w)* Separating the bulls

4.4 Translating the captions on BM EA 101:

Centre:

ptr nfrw nṯr nfr	Seeing the splendour of the perfect god
ḫꜥ-kꜣw-rꜥ mꜣꜥ-ḫrw	Khakaure, the justified,
mry wp-wꜣwt nb tꜣ-ḏsr	beloved of Wepwawet, lord of the sacred land
mry ꜣsir wnn-nfr nb ꜣbḏw	beloved of Osiris-Wenennefer, lord of Abydos.

Right:

dwꜣ wp-wꜣwt m prt=f nfrt	Adoring Wepwawet during his wonderful procession
ḏt r nḥḥ	enduringly and repeatedly.

Left:

dwꜣ ꜣsir m ḥb(w)=f nfrw	Adoring Osiris during his wonderful festivals
ḏt r nḥḥ	enduringly and repeatedly.

4.5 Translating the captions on BM EA 581

Top:

sn tꜣ n ḫnty-imntw	Kissing the ground to Khentyimentu
mꜣꜣ nfrw wp-wꜣwt	and seeing the splendour of Wepwawet
in m-r ꜥḫnwty intf	by the overseer of the chamber Intef.

Bottom:

prt-ḫrw n imꜣḫ(w)	A voice-offering for the revered one
m-r ꜥḫnwty intf ir-n snt	the overseer of the chamber Intef, born of Senet.

4.6 Study exercise: Fishing and fowling scene from the tomb of Senbi at Meir

Left-hand scene:

stt rm(w)	Spearing fish
ỉn ỉmꜣḫy ḫr ꜣsỉr nb smyt ỉmntt	by the revered one before Osiris, lord of the western desert,
ḥꜣty-ꜥ m-r ḥm-nṯr	the governor and overseer of the priests
snbỉ mꜣꜥ-ḫrw	Senbi, the justified.

Right-hand scene:

ꜥmꜥꜣ r ꜣpd(w)	Throwing at birds
ỉn ḥꜣty-ꜥ ḫtmty-bỉty	by the governor, seal-bearer of the king,
smr wꜥty snbỉ mꜣꜥ-ḫrw	and sole companion Senbi, the justified.

Above Senbi's wife:

ḥmt=f n st-ỉb=f	His wife of his affection
mrs nbt ỉmꜣḫ	Meres, possessor of reverence.

4.7 Study exercise: The coffin of Nakhtankh (BM EA 35285)

Eastern side – horizontal inscription:

ḥtp-dỉ-nsw	An offering which the king gives
ꜣsỉr nb ḏdw ḫnty-ỉmntw	to Osiris, lord of Djedu, Khentyimentu,
nṯr ꜥꜣ nb ꜣbḏw	great god, lord of Abydos,
dỉ=f ḫt nb(t) nfrt wꜥbt	so that he may give everything good and pure:
ḫꜣ m t ḥnḳt	a thousand of bread and beer,
kꜣ ꜣpd šs mnḫt	ox and fowl, alabaster and linen,
ꜥnḫt nṯr ỉm	on which a god lives,
n kꜣ n ỉmꜣḫ(y)	for the ka of the revered one,
nḫt-ꜥnḫ mꜣꜥ-ḫrw	Nakhtankh, the justified.

Vertical inscriptions from north to south:

ỉmꜣḫ(y) ḫr ỉmstỉ nḫt-ꜥnḫ	The revered one before Imseti, Nakhtankh.
ỉmꜣḫ(y) ḫr šw nḫt-ꜥnḫ mꜣꜥ-ḫrw	The revered one before Shu, Nakhtankh, the justified.
ỉmꜣḫ(y) ḫr gb nḫt-ꜥnḫ mꜣꜥ-ḫrw	The revered one before Geb, Nakhtankh, the justified.
ỉmꜣḫ(y) ḫr dwꜣ-mwt=f nḫt-ꜥnḫ mꜣꜥ-ḫrw	The revered one before Duamutef, Nakhtankh, the justified.

Western side – horizontal inscription:

ḥtp-dỉ-nsw	An offering which the king gives
ỉnp(w) ḫnty sḥ-nṯr	to Anubis, the one before the divine booth,
tp(y)-ḏw=f ỉm(y)-wt	the one on his mountain, the one in the *wt*,
nb tꜣ-ḏsr	lord of the sacred land:
ḳrst nfrt m ỉs=f nfr n ḫrt-nṯr	a good burial in his wonderful tomb of the necropolis;
ỉmꜣḫy ḫr nṯr ꜥꜣ	the revered one before the great god,
nḫt-ꜥnḫ mꜣꜥ-ḫrw	Nakhtankh, the justified.

Vertical inscriptions from north to south:

ỉmꜣḫ(y) ḫr ḥpy nḫt-ꜥnḫ mꜣꜥ-ḫrw	The revered one before Hapy, Nakhtankh, the justified.
ỉmꜣḫ(y) ḫr tfnt nḫt-ꜥnḫ mꜣꜥ-ḫrw	The revered one before Tefnut, Nakhtankh, the justified.
ỉmꜣḫ(y) ḫr nwt nḫt-ꜥnḫ mꜣꜥ-ḫrw	The revered one before Nut, Nakhtankh, the justified.
ỉmꜣḫ(y) ḫr ḳbḥ-snw=f nḫt-ꜥnḫ mꜣꜥ-ḫrw	The revered one before Qebehsenuef, Nakhtankh, the justified.

Chapter 5

5.2 Words:

	*ḥst*		*ẖnms*
	*ḏꜣt*		*wḏꜣ*
	*ḥḳꜣ*	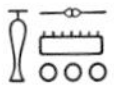	*ḥsmn*
	*nmtt*		*iwit*
	*ḏꜣ(i)*		

5.3 Translation:

a.	*iw ir.n=i prt ꜥꜣt*	I conducted the great procession.
b.	*iw ḳrs.n=i iꜣ(w)*	I buried the old.
c.	*iw rdi.n(=i) t n ḥḳr ḥbsw n ḥꜣy*	I gave bread to the hungry and clothes to the naked.
d.	*iw ḏꜣ.n(=i) iww <m> mẖnt(=i) ḏs(=i)*	I ferried the boatless in my own ferry.
e.	*iw wḥm.n(=i) ḥst ẖr nsw*	I repeated favour before the king.

5.4 Study exercise: BM EA 1783

Lines 1-2:

ḥtp-di-nsw	An offering which the king gives
inpw tp(y)-ḏw=f	to Anubis, the one on his mountain,
im(y)-wt nb tꜣ-ḏsr	the one in the *wt*, lord of the sacred land:
prt-ḫrw n ḥꜣty-ꜥ	a voice offering for the governor,
ḫtmty-bity smr-wꜥt(y)	seal-bearer of the king, sole companion,
ẖry-ḥbt	and lector-priest,
imꜣḫw ḫr nṯr ꜥꜣ nb pt	and revered one before the great god and lord of the sky,
in-ḥrt-nḫt ḏd	Inhuretnakht, who says:

Lines 4-5:

iw rdi.n(=i) t n ḥḳr	I gave bread to the hungry
ḥbsw n ḥꜣy	and clothes to the naked.
iw ḏꜣ.n(=i) iww <m> mẖnt(=i) ḏs(=i)	I ferried the boatless in my own ferry.
iw ir.n(=i) kꜣ(w) 100 m irt.n(=i) ḏs(=i)	I acquired 100 bulls through what I did myself.

The family:

ḥmt=f mrt=f ẖkrt-nsw wꜥtt	His beloved wife, the sole lady-in-waiting
ḥm(t)-nṯr ḥwt-ḥr	and priestess of Hathor,
imꜣḫt ḥwi	the revered one Hui.
sꜣ=f mry=f nnwy	His beloved son Nenwy.

The dedication:

irt.n n=f sꜣ=f smsw=f mry=f dbi	What his beloved eldest son Debi made for him.

5.5 Study exercise: BM EA 571 (top)

First offering formula:

ḥtp-di-nsw	An offering which the king gives
ꜣsir nb ḏdw ḫnty-imntw	to Osiris, lord of Djedu, Khentyimentu,
nṯr ꜥꜣ nb ꜣbḏw	great god, lord of Abydos,
di=f prt-ḫrw t ḥnḳt	so that he may give a voice offering of bread and beer,

ḫꜣ m kꜣ ꜣpd šs mnḫt	a thousand of ox and fowl, alabaster and linen,
ḫt nb(t) nfr(t) wꜥb(t)	and everything good and pure
ꜥnḫt nṯr ꜥꜣ ꞽm	on which the great god lives
n ꞽmꜣḫ(w) rḫ-nsw mry nb=f	for the revered one, king's advisor beloved of his lord,
m-r pr sꜣ-ḥwt-ḥr mꜣꜥ-ḫrw	the steward Sahathor, the justified,
ḥmt=f mrt=f ḫw	(and) his beloved wife Khu.

(the formula is finished off by the inscriptions above the figures of Sahathor and Khu)

Offering-bearers:

sꜣ=f mry=f m-r pr sꜣ-mnḫt mꜣꜥ-ḫrw	His beloved son, the steward Samenkhet, the justified.
m-r st ꞽntf	The overseer of the storehouse Intef.
wbꜣ m-sꜣ=f	The cup-bearer Emsaf.

Second offering formula:

ḥtp-dꞽ-nsw	An offering which the king gives
ꜣsꞽr nb ꞽmnt nfrt	to Osiris, lord of the beautiful west,
nṯr ꜥꜣ nb ꜣbḏw	great god, lord of Abydos,
dꞽ=f mw ḥnḳt snṯr mrḥt	so that he may give water and beer, incense and unguent
ḫt nb(t) nfr(t) wꜥb(t)	and everything good and pure
ꜥnḫt nṯr ꞽm	on which a god lives
m ꜣbd m ?-nt	in the month-festival, in the half-month festival
wꜣg ḏḥwtt	the Wag-festival and the Thoth-festival
ḏꜣt nṯr r pḳr	and the (festival of) the god's boat-journey to Poker
n ꞽmꜣḫ(w) m-r pr sꜣ-ꞽmn mꜣꜥ-ḫrw	for the revered one, the steward Saamun, the justified,
ḥmt=f mrt=f ḫw	(and) his beloved wife Khu.

(once again the formula is finished off by the inscriptions above the figures of Saamun and Khu)

Offering-bearers:

wbꜣ sḥtp-ꞽb	The cup-bearer Sehetepib.
ḫnms=f mry=f ꞽntf	His beloved friend Intef.

5.6 Study Exercise: BM EA 571 (bottom)

Transliteration and Translation:
a. Family:

sꜣ=f mry=f ꞽmny	His beloved son Ameny.
ḥmt=f mrt=f sꜣt-wsr(t)	His beloved wife Satwosret.
sꜣ=f mry=f ḥm-nṯr s-n-wsrt	His beloved son the priest Senwosret.
ḥmt=f mrt=f sꜣt-mnṯw	His beloved wife Satmentju.
sꜣ=f mry=f m-r pr ꞽmn-m-ḥꜣt	His beloved son the steward Amenemhet.
mwt=f bt	His mother Bet.

You may have noticed that the use of 'his' renders the precise reconstruction of genealogies rather problematic. Here the male figures are given in relation to either Sahathor or Saamun (the principal male figures in the offering scenes above), whereas the pairing of male and female figures seems to relate the females to their accompanying male figure rather than directly to either Sahathor or Saamun.
b. Household and estate:

šmsw ṯꜣw	The attendant Tjau.	*wbꜣt ḥtp*	The cup-bearer Hetep.
ḫrt-pr ḫw	The domestic Khu.	*ꜥḳ(y)t ddt*	The entering-maid Dedet.
sftw sꜣ-ḥwt-ḥr	The butcher Sahathor.	*rḫty sꜣ-ḥwt-ḥr*	The washerman Sahathor.

Chapter 6

6.2 Words:

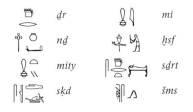

	*ḏr*		*mỉ*
	*nḏ*		*ḫsf*
	*mỉty*		*sḏrt*
	*sḳd*		*šms*

6.3 Translation:

a.	*ỉw*	*ḳrs.n=ỉ ỉꜣ(w)*	I	buried the old,
		ḥbs.n=ỉ ḥꜣy		I clothed the naked,
		n ỉr(=ỉ) ỉwỉt r rmṯ		and I did no wrong against people.
b.	*ỉw*	*dỉ.n(=ỉ) t n ḥḳr*	I	gave bread to the hungry
		ḥbs(w) n ḥꜣy		and clothes to the naked;
		n srḫ(=ỉ) ꜥꜣ(w)		I did not complain about the great,
		sḳbḥ.n(=ỉ) nḏs(w)		and I put the lowly at (their) ease.
c.	*ỉw*	*sꜥꜣ.n=f w(ỉ)*	He	advanced me,
		sḫnt.n=f st(=ỉ)		he promoted my position,
		dỉ.n=f w(ỉ) m st ḫrt-ỉb=f		and placed me in his confidence
		m ꜥḥ=f n wꜥꜥw		in his private palace (palace of privacy).

6.4 Translation:

ỉw=ỉ ḥr mꜥḳ ḏr pꜣt	I have been roasting since the beginning of time -
n mꜣ=ỉ mỉty srw pn	I have never seen the like of this goose.

6.5 Study exercise: The Osiris Mysteries at Abydos:

a. Transliteration and Translation

1	*ỉw*	*ỉr.n=ỉ prt wp-wꜣwt*	I	conducted the procession of Wepwawet,
		wḏꜣ=f r nḏ ỉt=f		when he set out to protect his father;
		ḫsf.n=ỉ sbỉ(w) ḥr nšmt		I drove away the rebels at the Neshmet-bark;
		sḫr.n=ỉ ḫft(w) ꜣsỉr		and I felled the enemies of Osiris.
	ỉw	*ỉr.n=ỉ prt ꜥꜣt*	I	conducted the great procession,
		šms=ỉ nṯr r nmtt=f		following the god at his travels;
		dỉ.n=ỉ sḳd dpt-nṯr		and I made the god's boat sail.
2	*ỉw*	*ḏsr.n=ỉ wꜣ(w)t nṯr*	I	cleared the ways of the god
		r mꜥḥꜥt=f ḫntt pḳr		to his tomb at the forefront of Poker.
	ỉw	*nḏ.n=ỉ wnn-nfr*	I	protected Wenennefer
		hrw pf n ꜥḥꜣ ꜥꜣ		on that day of the great fight;
		sḫr.n=ỉ ḫft(w)=f nb		I felled all his enemies
		ḥr ṯsw n ndyt		on the bank of Nedyet
		dỉ.n=ỉ wḏꜣ=f r ẖnw wrt		and I had him proceed inside the great bark.
3		*ỉn.n=s ꜣsỉr ḫnty-ỉmntw*	(and)	it brought Osiris Khentyimentu
		nb ꜣbḏw n ꜥḥ=f		lord of Abydos to his palace,
		šms.n=ỉ nṯr r pr=f		and I followed the god to his house.

6.6 Study exercise: BM EA 586

a. Text:

rnpt-sp 14 ḫr ḥm n nsw-bỉty	Year 14 under the person of the king of Upper and Lower
ḫpr-kꜣ-rꜥ ꜥnḫ ḏt	Egypt Kheperkare living forever.
ỉmꜣḫ(w) ỉt-nṯr ỉty ḏd=f	The revered one, the god's father Ity says:
ỉw wḥm.n(=ỉ) ḥst ḫr nsw	I repeated favour before the king
sꜥꜣ ỉb(=ỉ) r ỉt(w)(=ỉ)	and advanced my heart more than my forefathers
ḫprw r-ḥꜣt=ỉ	who existed before me.
ỉw ṯs.n -n=ỉ ḥm=f ḫtm ꜥꜣ	His person assigned to me a great seal
m ḥsmn wꜥb	in pure amethyst,
mỉ šps-nsw nb	just like any dignitary of the king,
ꜣryt=ỉ m hbny swꜥbt m ḏꜥm	and my staff in ebony decorated in electrum.
ỉmꜣḫ(w) ỉt-nṯr ỉty	The revered one, the god's father Ity.
ḥmt=f mrt=f ỉwrỉ	His beloved wife Iuri.

b. The family:

sꜣ=f ỉntf	His son Intef.
sꜣ=f ỉmn-m-ḥꜣt	His son Amenemhet.
sꜣt=f sꜣt-sbk	His daughter Satsobek.
sꜣt=f sꜣt-wsrt	His daughter Satwosret.

Chapter 7

7.2 Words:

 *nḏm*  *ḳmꜣ*

 *ḫr*  *wḏ*

 *nḫt*

7.4 Translation:

a. *ỉnk nḏs ỉḳr*	I was an astute individual
ḏd m r=f	who spoke with his (own) mouth,
ỉr m ḫpš=f	who acted with his (own) strong arm,
sḫsf nwt=f r=f	and who kept his town at a distance from himself.
ỉnk šps m wꜣst	I was a dignitary in Thebes,
ỉwn ꜥꜣ m ḫntyt	and a great pillar in Khentyt.
ỉw swꜣ.n(=ỉ) mỉty(=ỉ) nb	I surpassed any peer of mine
m nwt tn m špss nb	in this town in all kinds of dignity/wealth.

b. *bꜣk=f mꜣꜥ n st-ỉb=f*	His true servant of his affection,
ḫnt(y) st m pr nb=f	one foremost of position in the house of his lord;
sr ꜥꜣ n ỉb=f	an official great of his heart,
rḫ ḫrt-ỉb nb=f	one who knows the desire of his lord,
šms sw r nmtt=f nb(t)	one who follows him at all his journeys.

7.5 Stela of Ity (BM EA 586):

ỉmꜣḫ(w) ỉt-nṯr mry nb=f mꜣꜥ	The revered one the god's father, one truly beloved of his lord,
ḥry-sštꜣ n ỉmn-rꜥ m st=f nb	the master of secrets of Amun-Ra in any place of his,
ỉty ms-n sꜣt-sbk	Ity born of Satsobek.

(honorific transposition of *nb=f* 'his lord')

7.6 Relative forms:

ddt pt ḳmꜣt tꜣ	which the sky gives, which the land creates,
innt ḥꜥpy	and which the inundation brings.

7.7 Study exercise: BM EA 558

ḥtp-di-nsw	An offering which the king gives
ꜣsir nb ḏdw nṯr ꜥꜣ nb ꜣbḏw	to Osiris, lord of Djedu, great god, lord of Abydos,
di=f prt-ḫrw	so that he may give a voice offering of
t ḥnḳt kꜣ ꜣpd šs mnḫt	bread and beer, ox and fowl, alabaster and linen,
ḫt nb(t) nfr(t) wꜥb(t) ꜥnḫt nṯr im	and everything good and pure on which a god lives
n kꜣ n imꜣḫ(w) ky	for the ka of the revered one Key,
rḫ-nsw mꜣꜥ mry=f	a true king's adviser beloved of him
ir ḥst nsw	who has done what the king has favoured
m ẖrt-hrw nt rꜥ nb	during the course of every day.
ii(.n=i) m nwt(=i)	I have come from my town;
hꜣ.n(=i) m spꜣt(=i)	I have descended from my district.
ink ḏd nfrt	I was one who said what is good,
wḥm mrrt ḫrp rḫ-nsw	and who repeated what the director of king's advisers loves.
n ḏws(=i) s n ḥry-tp=f	I did not denounce a man to his superior;
n wḏ(=i) ḥwt m s=i	I did not command a beating for a man of mine.
imꜣḫ(w) ḫr nṯr ꜥꜣ	The revered one before the great god
wḥm ky ms-n mrti mꜣꜥ-ḫrw	the reporter Key, born of Merti, the justified.
dbḥt-ḥtp	Required offerings

7.8 Study exercise: BM EA 143

ḥtp-di-nsw	An offering which the king gives
ꜣsir nb ḏdw nṯr ꜥꜣ nb ꜣbḏw	to Osiris, lord of Djedu, great god, lord of Abydos,
di=f prt-ḫrw	so that he may give a voice offering of
t ḥnḳt kꜣ ꜣpd šs mnḫt	bread and beer, ox and fowl, alabaster and linen,
ḫt nbt nfrt wꜥbt ꜥnḫt nṯr im	and everything good and pure on which a god lives,
ddt pt ḳmꜣt tꜣ	which the sky gives, which the land creates,
innt ḥꜥp(y)	and which the innundation brings
m ḥtp-di-nsw	as an offering which the king gives,
ṯw n ꜥnḫ nḏm st snṯr wꜥb	the sweet breath of life, and the scent of pure incense
n kꜣ n ḥꜣty-ꜥ nḫti mꜣꜥ-ḫrw	for the ka of the governor Nakhti, the justified,
ms-n nḫti mꜣꜥt-ḫrw	born of Nakhti, the justified.

Below (from right to left):

ḥmt=f nbt-pr nt-nbw mꜣꜥt-ḫrw	His wife, the mistress of the house Netnebu, the justified.
mwt=f nbt-pr nḫti mꜣꜥt-ḫrw	His mother, the mistress of the house Nakhti, the justified.
mnꜥt ꜣst	The wet-nurse Iset.

Chapter 8

8.2 Words:

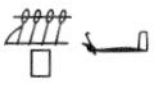	*šsp*		*sꜣḫ*
	*mꜥḥꜥt*		*šnyt*
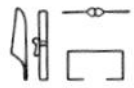	*is*		*ꜣḫ*

8.3 BM EA 567:

rnpt-sp 13 ḫr ḥm n	Regnal year 13 under the person of
nsw-bity nbw-kꜣw-rꜥ	the king of Upper and Lower Egypt Nubkaure,
di ꜥnḫ ḏt r nḥḥ	given life enduringly and repeatedly.
ḥtp-di-nsw	An offering which the king gives
ꜣsir nb ḏdw ḫnty-imntw nb ꜣbḏw	to Osiris, lord of Djedu, Khentyimentu, lord of Abydos
wp-wꜣwt ḫnty ꜣbḏw	and Wepwawet, the one at the forefront of Abydos,
ḥḳt ḥnꜥ ḫnmw	Heket and Khnum
nṯrw nb ꜣbḏw	and all the gods of Abydos
di=sn prt-ḫrw	so that they may give a voice offering of
t ḥnḳt kꜣ ꜣpd šs mnḫt	bread and beer, ox and fowl, alabaster and linen,
ḫt nbt nfr(t) pr(r)t m-bꜣḥ nṯr ꜥꜣ	and everything good which goes before the great god.
ms.t(w) n=f ꜥwy ḫr ḥtp	May hands be presented to him carrying offerings
m ḥb(w) nw ḫrt-nṯr	during the festivals of the necropolis
ḥnꜥ šms(w) n ꜣsir	along with the followers of Osiris,
tp(w)-ꜥ ḫprw ḫr-ḥꜣt	the ancestors who existed before.
sꜣḫ ṯw wr(w) nw ḏdw	May the great ones of Djedu
šnyt imt ꜣbḏw	and the entourage in Abydos enspirit you.
ḏd.t(w) n=f iiw m ḥtp	May 'Welcome in peace' be said to him
in wrw nw ꜣbḏw	by the great ones of Abydos.
sḏꜣ=f ḥnꜥ nṯr ꜥꜣ	May he travel with the great god
m ḏꜣt-nṯr r r-pḳr	during the god's journey to Ro-Poker,
nšmt wrt r nmtt=s	when the great Neshmet-bark is at its journeys
m ḥb(w) nw ḫrt-nṯr	during the festivals of the necropolis.
sdm=f hnw m r n tꜣ-wr	May he hear jubilation in the mouth of Tawer
hꜣkr grḥ n sḏrt	(at) the Haker-rites of the night of vigil
m sḏryt nt ḥr-šn	during the vigil of Horus-*šn*.

8.4 Study exercise: BM EA 584

ḥtp-di-nsw	An offering which the king gives
ꜣsir nb ḏdw ḫnty-imntw	to Osiris, lord of Djedu, Khentyimentu
<nṯr> ꜥꜣ nb ꜣbḏw	great (god), lord of Abydos,
wp-wꜣwt nb tꜣ ḏsr	Wepwawet, lord of the sacred land,
ḫnmw ḥnꜥ ḥḳt	Khnum and Heket
nṯrw nbw smyt imntt	and all the gods of the western desert,
di=sn prt-ḫrw	so that they may give a voice offering of
t ḥnḳt kꜣ ꜣpd šs mnḫt	bread and beer, ox and fowl, alabaster and linen,
ḥtp ḏf(ꜣw)	offerings and provisions
n kꜣ n imꜣḫ(w)	for the ka of the revered one
m-r iḳdw(w) ḫw-n-bik ḏd	the overseer of builders Khunenbik, who says:
i ꜥnḫw swꜣt(y).sn ḫr mꜥḥꜥt tn	O the living who may pass by this tomb
m ḫd m ḫsft	in going north or in going south,
m mrr=ṯn šms wp-wꜣwt r nmtt=f nb	as you wish to follow Wepwawet at all his journeys,
ḏd=ṯn t ḥnḳt ḫꜣ kꜣ ꜣpd ḫꜣ	may you say: 'Bread and beer, 1000, ox and fowl, 1000,
šs mnḫt ḫꜣ ḥtp ḏf(ꜣw) ḫꜣ	alabaster and linen, 1000, offerings and provisions, 1000,
m ḫt nbt nfrt wꜥbt ꜥnḫt nṯr im	as everything good and pure on which a god lives
n kꜣ n imꜣḫy ḫr nṯr(w) nb(w) ꜣbḏw	for the ka of the revered one before all the gods of Abydos
ḫr nsw	and before the king,

m-r iḳdw(w) ḫw-n-bik mꜣꜥ-ḫrw	the overseer of builders Khuenbik, the justified,
ms-n rrwt	born of Rerut'.

The family:

ḥmt=f ḥwt-ḥr ms(t)-n mꜣi-n-ḥr	His wife Hathor, born of Mainenhor.
sꜣt=f rrw(t) mꜣꜥ(t)-ḫrw	His daughter Rerut, the justified.
in sꜣ=f sꜥnḫ rn=f	It is his son who has made his name live (on)
m-r iḳdw(w) n-ptḥ-kꜣ(w)	the overseer of builders Niptahkau.
sꜣ=f mry=f ptḥ-ḥtp	His beloved son Ptahhotep.

8.5 Study exercise: BM EA 162

ḥtp-di-nsw	An offering which the king gives/places
ḫr ꜣsir ḫnty-imntw	before Osiris-Khentyimentu,
[nṯr ꜥꜣ nb] ꜣbḏw	[great god, lord] of Abydos
m s(w)t=f nbt nfrt wꜥbt	in all his good and pure places,
di=f prt-ḫrw	so that he may give a voice offering
m t m ḥnḳt	in bread and in beer
m kꜣ ꜣpd m ḫt nb(t) nfrt	in ox and fowl and in everything good
n kꜣ n imꜣḫw ḫr nṯr ꜥꜣ	for the ka of the revered one before the great god,
m-r mšꜥ wr imny	the general-in-chief Ameny,
ir-n ḳbw mꜣꜥ-ḫrw	born of Kebu, the justified.
di.t(w) n=f ꜥwy m nšmt	May help be given to him in the Neshmet-bark
ḥr wꜣ(w)t imnt	on the ways of the West.
šsp=f ḥtpt ḥr ḥtp ꜥꜣ	May he receive offerings (from) upon the great altar
m ḥb(w) n ẖrt-nṯr	during the festivals of the necropolis.
ḏd.t(w) n=f iw m ḥtp	May 'Welcome in peace' be said to him
in wr(w) n ꜣbḏw	by the great ones of Abydos
m wꜣg m ḏḥwtt	at the Wag-festival, at the Thoth-festival,
m ḥb-skr m prt-mnw	at the Soker-festival, at the procession of Min,
m prt spdt m tp-rnpt	at the procession of Sothis, at the begining of the lunar year,
m ḥb(w) nb ꜥꜣ irrw	and at all the great festivals which are performed
n ꜣsir ḫnty-imntw nṯr ꜥꜣ	for Osiris-Khentyimentu, the great god,
n kꜣ n m-r mšꜥ wr imny	for the ka of the general-in-chief Ameny

Family, colleagues and staff in central scene:

ḥmt=f mrt=f	His beloved wife
irrt ḥsst=f rꜥ nb	who does what he favours every day
ḥm(t)-nṯr ḥwt-ḥr mdḥw	the priestess of Hathor Medhu,
mst-n imny mꜣꜥt-ḫrw	born of Ameny, the justified.
wbꜣt sꜣt-ḫnt-ḫty	The cup-bearer Satkhenetkhety.
bꜣk=f mꜣꜥ n st-ib=f	His true servant of his affection,
irr ḥsst=f rꜥ nb	who does what he favours every day
m-r ḫtmt sꜣ-ḥwt-ḥr	the treasurer Sahathor,
nb imꜣḫ mꜣꜥ-ḫrw	possessor of reverence, the justfied.
sn=f mr(y)=f ḫnt-ḫty-ḥtp	His beloved brother Khenetkhetyhetep
ir-n sꜣt-sbk mꜣꜥ-ḫrw	born of Satsobek, the justified.

Lower scene:

sꜣ-ḫnt-ḫty	Sakhenetkhety.
ḥm-kꜣ ḏfꜣ-ḥꜥp(y)	The ka-priest Djefahapy.
nšt ḫwyt	the hairdresser Khuyet.
ḥr(y)-pr imny	The domestic Ameny.
ḥr(y)-pr sꜣwtyt	The domestic Sautyt.

Bibliography and further reading

The following bibliography is highly selective and aimed at works which will supplement this book and aid you in further reading and study. We have tried to concentrate on books which are still in print and available through major stockists. However, some works of particular relevance for the topics covered in this book will probably only be found in specialist libraries and these are prefixed with *.

Hieroglyphs

On hieroglyphs, two books in particular can be recommended to complement the early part of this book:

W.V. Davies, *Egyptian Hieroglyphs,* Reading the Past series, British Museum Press, London 1987.

J. Malek, *ABC of Egyptian Hieroglyphs,* Ashmolean Museum, Oxford 1994.

Kings' names

A fuller list of the cartouches of the kings of Egypt can be found in:

S.J. Quirke, *Who were the Pharaohs? A History of their Names with a List of their Cartouches,* British Museum Press, London 1990.

Stelae

If you are interested in extending your reading of stelae and coffins, then examples for study are on display in most major museums. In the UK, the following museums have particularly suitable collections (the list is not exhaustive and a number of other museums and private collections also have Middle Kingdom stelae and coffins on display):

Southern England: British Museum, London; Ashmolean Museum, Oxford; Fitzwilliam Museum, Cambridge.

Northern England: Merseyside County Museum, Liverpool; The Manchester Museum; The Oriental Museum, Durham.

Scotland: Royal Museum of Scotland, Edinburgh; Kelvingrove Art Gallery and Museum, Glasgow.

However, if you have access to a good specialist library (such as the library of the Egypt Exploration Society, open to members of the society) then the following two works contain a number of interesting stelae for study:

The most convenient collection of Abydos stelae remains:

* W.K. Simpson, *The Terrace of the Great God at Abydos: The Offering Chapels of Dynasties 12 and 13.*, Publications of the Pennsylvania–Yale Expedition to Egypt No. 5, Peabody Museum of Natural History and The University Museum of the University of Pennsylvania, New Haven and Philadelphia 1974.

(This book contains photographs of a number of Abydene Middle Kingdom stelae from museum collections around the world, including some of the stelae studied here, reassembled by Simpson into the original groups of monuments found at Abydos.)

The following title contains a number of stelae from Nagʿ ed-Deir of a similar kind to BM EA 1783 (p. 74):

* D. Dunham, *Naga-ed-Dêr stelae of the First Intermeditate Period,* Museum of Fine Arts, Boston 1937.

Coffins

A convenient introduction to coffins and their development is:

J.H. Taylor, *Egyptian Coffins,* Shire Publications, Aylesbury 1989.

A more detailed discussion of Middle Kingdom coffins can be found in:

* H.O. Willems, *Chests of Life: A Study of the Typology and Conceptual Development of Middle Kingdom Standard Class Coffins,* Orientaliste, Leuven 1988.

Religion: Osiris and the afterlife

A convenient recent account is provided in:

S.J. Quirke, *Ancient Egyptian Religion,* British Museum Press, London 1992 (especially Chapters 2 and 5).

Titles

There is no readily available general work on titles to aid you in your reading. However, a convenient listing of titles by function can be found in:

* S.J. Quirke, 'The regular titles of the late Middle Kingdom', *Revue d'Égyptologie* 37 (1986), pp. 107-30.

Otherwise, the major listing of Middle Kingdom titles with hieroglyphs, transliteration and translation is:

* W.A. Ward, *Index of Egyptian Administrative and Religious Titles of the Middle Kingdom, with a Glossary of Words and Phrases Used,* American University in Beirut Press, Beirut 1982.

Translations

The most convenient set of translations for Middle Kingdom stelae (which includes a number of, but far from all, the examples in this book) is:

* M. Lichtheim, *Ancient Egyptian Autobiographies chiefly of the Middle Kingdom: A Study and an Anthology*, Orbis Biblicus et Orientalis 84, Universitätsverlag, Freiburg and Vandenhoeck & Ruprecht, Göttingen 1988

Some stelae are also included in Lichtheim's earlier and more readily available book:

M. Lichtheim, *Ancient Egyptian Literature, 1: The Old and Middle Kingdoms*, University of California Press, Berkeley and Los Angeles 1973.

A more recent anthology of translations from a variety of Middle Kingdom texts, including stelae, is:

R.B. Parkinson, *Voices from Ancient Egypt. An Anthology of Middle Kingdom Writings*, British Museum Press, London 1991.

Dictionaries and sign-lists

The most convenient dictionary in English remains:

R.O. Faulkner, *A Concise Dictionary of Middle Egyptian*, Griffith Institute, Oxford 1962.

A more comprehensive sign-list with an extensive discussion of the use of signs is included at the end of:

A.H. Gardiner, *Egyptian Grammar, Being an Introduction to the Study of Hieroglyphs*. 3rd edition, Griffith Institute, Oxford 1957.

Both of these works are still in print and readily available.

Grammar

Gardiner's *Egyptian Grammar* also remains the most comprehensive treatment of ancient Egyptian in English, although a number of the sections on the verb (occupying the second half of the book) are now rather dated.

An up-to-date account in English of the grammar of Middle Kingdom texts can now be found in:

J.P. Allen, *Middle Egyptian. An Introduction to the Language and Culture of Hieroglyphs*. Cambridge University Press, Cambridge 2000.

Allen's book also has some useful sections on topics not covered in this book, such as other categories of ancient Egyptian literature, as well as a broader account of religion.

Our book is not intended as a grammar book, but lying behind the presentation of the language is the particular 'verbalist' approach developed by Mark Collier in a number of specialist papers. A similar 'verbalist' approach is conveniently presented in:

A. Loprieno, *Ancient Egyptian: A Linguistic Introduction*, Cambridge University Press, Cambridge 1995.

This book also provides a concise account of the historical development of ancient Egyptian language and scripts.

Index

Index of illustrations (monuments from the British Museum collection)